Crosscurrents / MODERN CRITIQUES

Harry T. Moore, *General Editor*

Heroic Fiction

The Epic Tradition and American Novels of the Twentieth Century

Leonard Lutwack

WITH A PREFACE BY
Harry T. Moore

SOUTHERN ILLINOIS UNIVERSITY PRESS
Carbondale and Edwardsville

FEFFER & SIMONS, INC.
London and Amsterdam

Contents

Preface

It is interesting to note that two of the novels chosen for examination in the present book, which discusses recent American fiction in the light of the epic tradition, are also dealt with in an earlier and quite different volume in the Crosscurrents/Modern Critiques series. This is Warren French's valuable study, published in 1965, of The Social Novel at the End of an Era, which among other items focused upon Hemingway's For Whom the Bell Tolls and Steinbeck's The Grapes of Wrath. Now we find them viewed from a quite different angle in Heroic Fiction: The Epic Tradition and American Novels of the Twentieth Century, also a valuable book, this one by Professor Leonard Lutwack of the University of Maryland. Besides Hemingway and Steinbeck, Mr. Lutwack also takes up the work of such recent novelists as Ralph Ellison and Saul Bellow. And there is the earlier Frank Norris, with The Octopus.

At the beginning of his book, Mr. Lutwack discusses not only earlier American writers who produced epics, such as Melville in Moby-Dick, but also the epic tradition in general, showing how "the epic tradition and the novel have been of mutual benefit, the deficiencies of one being corrected by the virtues of the other," and pointing out that "the tendency of epic writing to become bombastic is corrected by the novel's commitment to plain prose, while the triviality of the novel's facts is re-

lieved by the epic's elevated tone," points which Mr. Lutwack drives home effectively not only in his Introduction
but also in analyzing the novels in question.

He notes, in his discussion of For Whom the Bell
Tolls, that "the battle epic was a need of the 1930s which
prompted Steinbeck to write an epic novel of economic
strife and Hemingway an epic novel of war." Mr. Lutwack sees Hemingway's Lieutenant Henry of A Farewell
to Arms, Robert Jordan of For Whom the Bell Tolls,
and Colonel Cantwell of Across the River and Into the
Trees as "three American war heroes [who are] reflections
of the changing role of the United States in European
wars of the twentieth century. Lieutenant Henry could
then be taken to represent the partial commitment of
American forces in World War I; Jordan the total commitment, even to the point of cooperating with Communist allies, at the height of World War II; and Colonel Cantwell the growing disillusionment with Cold War
politics."

Elsewhere Mr. Lutwack points out that For Whom
the Bell Tolls contains more romantic interest than other
modern epics, and that this "serves a very important thematic purpose" since "Maria is much more than a lover
and survivor: she becomes the cause for which the partisans are fighting," symbolizing a purity and innocence.
The author makes out a careful case, though many Hemingway readers will still prefer the failed romance in A
Farewell to Arms, if only for the concision of its action
and language. Similarly, some of us who read Steinbeck
will prefer In Dubious Battle, today a most unfashion-
able novel, to The Grapes of Wrath with its Sandburg-
like choral effects and massive sentimentalism. Yet Mr.
Lutwack always makes his points neatly, and in all the
books under consideration he gives us important new
readings of their texts, for example indicating that The

Grapes of Wrath becomes less interesting toward its conclusion, but pointing out that this also applies to one of
its models, the Aeneid. Among American writers of the
epic, Steinbeck is directly in the line of Frank Norris,
whose Octopus Mr. Lutwack gives unusually full treatment, all the more useful since there are so few full critical discussions of this book. As Mr. Lutwack shows, Norris's "Wheat Series" (including The Octopus) was referred to from the first as epic; and he also demonstrates
how Norris himself was conscious of writing in the epic
vein; he had spoken of what he felt were epic qualities
in the French author he admired so much, Émile Zola.
Mr. Lutwack provides an interesting and relevant discussion of Norris's division of the epic hero into four different men in The Octopus, whose "grand theme" is "the
renewal of life." Admitting Norris's stylistic limitations,
Mr. Lutwack nevertheless finds him writing impressively
of the great wheat landscapes. He has given us important
new perspectives on this author.

He does likewise with Ralph Ellison, showing how the
hero of this writer's "black odyssey" undergoes various
phases of the death-and-rebirth theme in various technical approaches (realistic, expressionistic, surrealistic),
continually providing fresh insights into Ellison's endur-
ing book. In dealing in some detail with three of Saul
Bellow's novels (Seize the Day, Henderson the Rain
King, and Herzog), Mr. Lutwack discusses them as odysseys of different kinds exploring various phases of modern existence. It is good to find that Mr. Lutwack's book
includes Mr. Sammler's Planet, another odyssey of yet
another kind and, like its predecessors, one of the finest
examples of recent fiction; indeed, there has been no
other work in years that shows so excruciatingly what it
means to live in our hypertense world.

In subjecting all these novels to tests of epic elements,

*Leonard Lutwack has performed a valuable critical serv-
ice which will help its readers to see twentieth-century
fiction with a new and fuller understanding.*

HARRY T. MOORE
Southern Illinois University
February 17, 1971

Introduction

In the present state of literary criticism, to call a piece of writing "epic" can no longer be accepted as the assertion of merit it once was when genres were confidently arranged in a hierarchy in which the epic occupied the first rank. The manufacturer of floor wax may suggest the highest quality and best performance by naming his product Epic, but the literary critic cannot do the same for a book without yielding to the blurring of popular usage. For him the attribution of epic qualities to contemporary writing must be primarily a method of classification promising only to show the manner in which traditional forms and materials continue to be adapted. He assumes that all narrative writing uses some epic conventions and that some novels use more than others, and these he calls epic novels. He must admit that the novel that preserves certain themes and forms of the past, and does not treat them ironically, sets itself against the current of most contemporary fiction. In America the epic is even considered by some to be a distinctly uncharacteristic form. "American fiction has approximated the poetry of the idyl or of melodrama more often than of epic," Richard Chase believes.[1] According to E. M. W. Tillyard, the true American form is "the documentary novel" of Dreiser and Dos Passos, whose works are said to occupy a place in the history of American literature equivalent

to the annalists in Roman literature.[2] Yet novels drawing upon the epic have been written in America and
deserve identification as a minority tradition, if nothing
else. The absurdity of human behavior and the hero as
victim and outcast may better respond to our present
sense of reality, but the heroic self-sacrifice and the
persistent faith in purposeful action have also stirred the
imagination of some American novelists. The ironic use
of myth may be dominant when a realistic mode of
writing returns to myth, according to Northrop Frye,
but it should be remembered that at no time in the
endless cycle of literary fashions is the serious and
sympathetic treatment of myth ever abandoned. Even
in the heyday of naturalism, within the naturalistic
novel itself, the epic spirit persists.

American literature, R. W. B. Lewis observes, is "the
most *Western* of the literature of the Western world,"
revealing "an extravagant appetite for the whole range
of Western literature, philosophy, and theology, and for
seizing again upon the archetypal human dilemmas." [3]
But the manner in which the American writer absorbs
the past is not precise, Lewis remarks in another place,
offering Melville's practice as representative: "the traditional materials appear raggedly, they are lumpy and
not altogether digested." [4] Since little can be gained,
therefore, from tracing direct "influences," our objective
will be the elucidation of texts by fixing their relations
to a broad and varied stream of narrative art in which
the heroic, the mythic, and the transcendent are the
chief ingredients and of which the epic is the definitive
expression.

Just before World War II sentiment ran high for
works inspiring community effort to face economic and
political enemies. In England even the staid *Times Literary Supplement* was sufficiently aroused during the Battle
of Britain to call for epic writing. The leader for August

31, 1940, began: "This is a time for epic drama"; the following week's number repeated the call: "A stirring thrills the air. This is a time for epic." At that time in America, *The Grapes of Wrath*, following in the tradition of *The Octopus*, addressed itself to class warfare and *For Whom the Bell Tolls* to the war against fascism. After World War II, the odyssey epic was found to be a convenient form to portray the plight of the individual who was left isolated by the cessation of hostilities on both economic and military battlegrounds. "The whole world is an *Iliad*" in wartime, Glenway Wescott wrote in 1962; "in our present peacetime . . . the whole world is an *Odyssey*" and the question of "the way home" is being posed "more solemnly than it has ever been posed before, in song or story, in epic or in tragic drama." [5] In *Henderson the Rain King* the hero is discontent with the home he finds after returning from war and sets out again, this time on a journey to ease his spirit so that he can return home a second time; in *Invisible Man* the hero returns to his people in order to deliver them from the bondage of racial discrimination. Other battle epics and other odysseys are treated in less detail, but no attempt is made at comprehensiveness, the offered texts being illustrations of a broad tradition.

I would like to make the following acknowledgments for permission to quote passages from the works listed:

Excerpts from *Herzog* by Saul Bellow. Copyright © 1961, 1963, 1964 by Saul Bellow. Reprinted by permission of The Viking Press, Inc. and Weidenfeld & Nicolson Ltd. From *Henderson the Rain King* by Saul Bellow. Copyright © 1958, 1959 by Saul Bellow. Reprinted by permission of The Viking Press, Inc. and Weidenfeld & Nicolson Ltd. From *Seize the Day* by Saul

I also wish to express my gratitude to the General Research Board of the Graduate School, University of Maryland, for grants that afforded me uninterrupted time to do research and writing; to seminar students who tested my thesis on a wide range of American fiction; to Mrs. Carolyn Tranum for bringing the manuscript through its several revisions.

LEONARD LUTWACK

University of Maryland
April 1971

Heroic Fiction

1

History and Definition

To be fitted out as soon as possible with the accoutrements of Western civilization was an American desire from the very beginning of the colonial settlements. The call for epic poems written by American poets and celebrating the New World had become a critical commonplace by the time John Adams gave it succinct expression in 1785: "I should hope to see our young America in Possession of an Heroick Poem, equal to those esteemed in any Country." [1] Poems answering the call duly appeared, in 1787 Joel Barlow's *The Vision of Columbus* (later revised and entitled *The Columbiad*) and Richard Snowden's *The Columbiad* in 1795. But an American imitation of ancient epics is found even earlier and, surprisingly, in a prose work, Cotton Mather's *Magnalia Christi Americana* (1702). To Mather the history of the Puritan church in the colonies and the lives of its outstanding leaders were noble enough subject to be embellished with traditional epic tags. These are clustered in the General Introduction, where the author is intent upon establishing the importance of his subject; epic form and tone hardly influence the bulk of the work, which Whittier described as a collection of "strange and marvellous things, heaped up huge and undigested." The *Magnalia* begins with the customary announcement of the subject and invocation to the Muse:

I write the Wonders of the CHRISTIAN RE-LIGION, flying from the Depravations of Europe, to the American Strand: And, assisted by the Holy Author of that Religion, I do, with all Conscience of Truth, required therein by Him, who is the Truth it self, Report the Wonderful Displays of His Infinite Power, Wisdom, Goodness, and Faithfulness, where-with His Divine Providence hath Irradiated an Indian Wilderness.

Then comes the traditional epic question in the form of a quotation from book 1 of the *Aeneid*: "The Reader will doubtless desire to know, what it was that *tot Volvere casus . . . impulerit*." Mather anticipates the objection that church history does not make suitable material for heroic treatment with the claim that "The Atchievements of one Paul . . . have more True Glory in them, than all the Acts of those Execrable Plunderers and Murderers, and irresistible Banditti of the World, which have been dignified with the Name of Conquerors." This is in the same spirit as Milton's disavowal of warlike subjects in book 9 of *Paradise Lost*; Joel Barlow repeats the formula in the preface of his *Columbiad* when he claims that "the real object" of the poem "is to inculcate the love of rational liberty, and to discountenance the deleterious passion for violence and war." Whitman picks up the refrain sixty-five years later in his "Song of the Exposition":

> Ended for aye the epics of Asia's, Europe's helmeted
>   warriors, ended the primitive call of the muses . . .
> The Crusaders' streams of shadowy midnight troops
>   sped with the sunrise . . .

It remained for Emerson, in his essay "The Poet," to state the case of the American epic most emphatically:

Banks and tariffs, the newspaper and caucus, methodism and unitarianism, are flat and dull to dull people, but rest on the same foundations of wonder as the town of Troy, and the temple of Delphos, and are as swiftly passing away. Our logrolling, our stumps and their politics, our fisheries, our Negroes, and Indians, our boasts and our repudiations, the wrath of rogues, and the pusillanimity of honest men, the northern trade, the southern planting, the western clearing, Oregon and Texas, are yet unsung. Yet America is a poem in our eyes; its ample geography dazzles the imagination, and it will not wait long for metres.

American writers are no exception to the practice which each age reserves for itself of claiming contemporary subjects to be worthier of epic treatment than those of the past. "The great paradox of the epic," writes a recent student of the form, "lies in the fact that the partial repudiation of earlier epic tradition is itself traditional." [2] The implication of Camoens that the theater of his hero's exploits (the Atlantic and Indian oceans) makes Homer's Mediterranean look like a pond is echoed across centuries and continents by the assertion of an American biographer that "Kit Carson's endless journeys through the wilderness make the fabled Mediterranean wanderings of Odysseus seem week-end excursions of a stay-at-home." [3]

Mather's treatment of native American materials in a prose narrative using epic conventions presages, at least in principle, the sub-genre which forms the subject of this study, the epic novel. Renaissance criticism conceded the possibility of epics in prose, and the association of epic with the writing of history and biography was common in the eighteenth century. But prose has never been the uncontested vehicle of epic, and few Americans who pondered the subject, even as late as the nineteenth century, would dare contravene the neo-classical predilection for heroic verse. Thus, not more

Magnalias were produced, but Barlow's, Trumbull's, and Snowden's dutiful long epic poems.

The ambition to write a great epic poem did not die with these unsuccessful attempts but reappears again and again in the literary history of the United States, and even in such an iconoclast as Whitman. Although he had to insist that "the expression of the American poet is to be transcendent and new," Whitman nonetheless thought of his *Leaves of Grass* as "an epic of Democracy" and incorporated in it familiar epic devices. Just as in *Magnalia*, it is at the very beginning of the work—in the first two poems—that epic conventions can be most readily found, such as the Virgilian announcement of his subject ("One's-self I sing"), the presence of the Muse ("A Phantom arose before me"), and the claim of having a new, superior subject—a war waged in his book—"For life and death, for the Body and for the eternal soul." Traditional epic themes may be found in the catalogues of American heroes (the common workmen of the land) and their occupations, the Civil War poems, the journey of the hero from the sea ("Starting from Paumanok" and "Out of the Cradle Endlessly Rocking") through the land of the dead ("When Lilacs Last in the Dooryard Bloom'd") to a mystical sense of identification with all people and things, all places and times. In establishing himself as the grand representative of the American personality, Whitman borrows colors from the epic hero; in justifying New World democracy, he becomes his own Aeneas. In this manner a case may be made to classify *Leaves of Grass* as an epic, but only at the cost of enlarging definitions and overlooking the book's lack of unity and narrative motifs and its intensely lyrical tone.[4] Whitman himself saw the difference between the *Iliad*, which he termed "notably objective," and his own "profoundly subjective" poems.[5]

Prose fiction inherited more of the epic tradition than poetry in the nineteenth century, first the prose of the romance and then, later in the century, the prose of the novel. In commenting on Mather's *Magnalia*, Moses Coit Tyler observes that "history and fiction are so jumbled and shuffled together, that it is never possible to tell . . . just where the fiction ends and the history begins." [6] Such might be the description of the historical romance developed in England by Scott and naturalized in this country by Cooper and William Gilmore Simms. It was Simms, in the preface of his *Yemassee*, who made the boldest claim for the new narrative form: "The modern Romance is the substitute which the people of the present day offer for the ancient epic." At a time when criticism was troubled by the distinction between the romance and the novel, epicness was considered one of the distinguishing features of romance.

The epic quality in the fiction of Cooper has often been noted and perhaps never stated in a more complimentary way than by the distinguished Marxist critic, Georg Lukács, when he said that "in the entire history of the novel" Cooper belongs in the company of Scott and Tolstoy for approaching "the character of the old epos." [7] If a case can be made for Scott, as E. M. W. Tillyard attempts to do,[8] one can be made for Cooper as well, but, as with Scott, no single work can stand up under scrutiny as an epic. The five Leatherstocking novels are comparable to the three border novels which Tillyard identifies as an "epic area." The decline of American Indians under the pressure of white settlers and the tragic mediation of Natty Bumppo make a subject of "epic grandeur." But Natty Bumppo, who would serve admirably as a hero's companion, does not command our deeper interest as a central figure, and Cooper's truly grand theme is unfortunately never his sole concern; the conventions of the sentimental novel and the adventure story crowd out whatever chance there was to develop his epic subject. Cooper's Leatherstocking, together with the little group of upper class whites, may touch the springs of heroic action in the pattern of separation, rescue, and reunion they endlessly repeat, but their involvement with this pattern is only melodramatic and sentimental.

To his illustrious predecessors' conception of the romance-epic William Gilmore Simms added a strong feeling of patriotism, a regional, Southern patriotism as compared to the national patriotism of Barlow and his contemporaries. American subjects and literary productions, Simms was convinced, can be as great as any: "The airy structures of our imagination, born of a like sky and atmosphere with that of Greece, should not shrink from comparison with those of Dodona and Hymettus." [9] Even the life of the American Indians could be the subject of great poetry:

> the thousand barbarian tribes by which these woods and wilds were traversed before the coming of our ancestors—their petty wars, their various fortunes, their capricious passions, their dark-eyed women, their favorite warriors—will, like those of Greece, be made immortal on the lips of eternal song. [10]

But it was the emergence of the South as a new nation that most inspired Simms and made the epic subject of many of his works. His conception of the epic and the means of execution at his disposal were inadequate, however, to produce a work of undoubted stature, and we must be content, on the admission of his best defenders, with snatches of epic writing "still salvageable from the body of his romances." [11] His own description of the kind of fiction he writes reveals the bizarre mixture of melodrama and myth so dear to him as well as to Cooper: in the same paragraph of the *Yemassee* preface in which the modern romance is claimed to be the substitute of ancient epic, he goes on to define romance: "placing a human agent in hitherto untried situations, it exercises its ingenuity in extricating him from them."

Cooper and Simms may have been inspired with truly epic subjects, but their chosen vehicle of composition, the romance, because of its easy hospitality towards sentimental and melodramatic forms, was not suited to the creation of epic quality. The effect of their themes is dissipated by competition from the sentimental interests of individuals in momentary distress; the force-fulness of direct action, so important in epic, is lost in the maze of intrigues. The unity of Cooper's work, especially, is further hampered by conflicting literary principles that he could never reconcile: the quarrel between the romancer and the realistic novelist on the one hand, and the conflict "between the epic writer and the writer of romance" on the other.[12] Cooper makes what resolution he can by alternating styles in the same work, a practice that opened him to the charge of Mark Twain, in "Fenimore Cooper's Literary Offenses," that a Cooper character often "talks like an illustrated, gilt-edged, tree-calf, hand-tooled, seven-dollar Friendship's Offering in the beginning of a paragraph [and] like a negro minstrel in the end of it."

Herman Melville, too, was torn by conflicting methods of literary expression and form, but he differs from Cooper in that the conflict is apparent within only two of his works, and in these it is not an awkward alternating of styles that he takes for his solution but the abrupt abandonment of one style in favor of another. *Mardi* begins as a novel and suddenly becomes an allegory; *Moby-Dick* again begins as a novel of a boy's seagoing experiences and becomes, in the words of D. H. Lawrence, an "epic of the sea."[13]

There is no need to go over the ground proving that

Moby-Dick owes much to the epic tradition. Most Melville critics make the observation, none more exhaustively and convincingly than Newton Arvin, who closes his discussion with a reminder that what makes *Moby-Dick* epic is its precise use of myth "in the sense of an imagined narrative in which the leading roles are played by divine or godlike personages, engaged in symbolic actions amid symbolic objects; which embodies some form of the conflict between human wishes and nonhuman forces, and which has its roots in a philosophically serious desire to comprehend the meaning of nature and the destiny of man." [14] The mythicizing, or whatever it is that makes *Moby-Dick* a rich and strange book, does not begin to make itself felt until the introduction of Ahab and his mad quest. Up to this point we have had a thoroughly novelistic piece of writing which follows with realistic fidelity, modulated slightly by a whimsical tone, the closely textured experience of Ishmael going down to the sea; but with Ahab's entry the epic or mythic strain takes hold. The result is that *Moby-Dick* is not a novel accommodating itself to the epic tradition, but rather a juxtaposition of a novel and a primary epic. The novelistic principles upon which the first twenty-seven chapters are constructed simply yield to the principles governing an imitation of a primary epic: the unheroic, ordinary character gives place to the heroic exotic who is "formed for noble tragedies"; credibility of plot and motivation give way to the fantastic and irrational; the continuum of existence so essential in the novel is dropped for the episodic structure of the epic; standard literary prose is transformed into the elevated language of Ahab's speeches. In yielding to another form, the novel Melville started to write is overwhelmed, and it is the epic quality of the whole book finally which makes the lasting impression. It is hard to remember, for instance, that Ishmael survives in the end. Melville was certainly successful in "liberating" his factual material from "novelistic restrictions," as Leslie Fiedler states, but in so doing he ended up, not with a novel, but with "the most improbable of all epic poems." [15]

Moby-Dick cannot be placed in the category of works that honor the novel form at the same time that they draw upon the epic tradition. Yet Melville's great masterpiece undoubtedly lies behind those works that do, the American epic novels of the twentieth century. It did introduce unequivocally the spirit of the epic to American fiction by daring to endow native materials with qualities of the heroic past, thus fulfilling specifically Emerson's proud assertion that "our fisheries . . . rest on the same foundation of wonder as the town of Troy." And *Moby-Dick* does fall in even with Whitman's hope for "an epic of Democracy" to the extent that Melville sees egalitarianism as a distinguishing feature of his book. Once the *Pequod* is under way, in chapter 26, and Melville has begun to take the full measure of his task, the narrator asks the "great democratic God," the "just spirit of Equality, which has spread one royal mantle of humanity over all my kind," to bear him out for ascribing heroic qualities "to meanest mariners, and renegades and castaways." Late as it is in the book, this is the traditional claim of distinction for a new epic subject and the invocation to a new kind of Muse. In the subsequent story of the captain and crew of a whaling ship Melville establishes for his American posterity the precedent of turning low materials to epic use. As developed by Melville, Ahab is one of the "kings of men for our Democracy" of whom Whitman speaks in his lecture on Lincoln: "more fateful than anything in Eschylus—more heroic than the fighters around Troy . . . prouder than Agamemnon— models of character cute and hardy as Ulysses—deaths more pitiful than Priam's." [16]

Although it is the "Spirit of Equality" that approves

of the use of common men in heroic roles, it could not have been a "democratic God" that inspired the tragic tone of *Moby-Dick*. After examining the marginal comments and underlinings made by Melville in his copies of Homer, R. W. B. Lewis observes that Melville dwelt upon "the griefs and hardships of Odysseus and the generalizations about the evil lot of mankind" and that the *Iliad* "emerges as the somber portrait of a world at war, of sorrowing men caught up in vast forces and moving without hope to the violent death which awaits them, under the rule of implacable divinities." [17] Julian N. Hartt is uneasy about the "dark epics" of Melville and Conrad because they present solitary heroes who have no "actual efficacy" in the community. [18] Lacking the sense of an ideal community, they contribute to "the death of the epic image" in modern times. It will remain to be seen whether one should despair so over the contemporary epic novel, yet it undoubtedly is the dark as well as the democratic epic of Melville that stands behind the twentieth-century epic novels we shall be examining, works that rival the general desolation of *Moby-Dick*'s ending. In spite of its New World origin the American epic novel does not ride on a Renaissance wave of ebullience and expansionism but rather in a storm of despondency, doubt, and universal destruction.

Primitivism is another quality of *Moby-Dick* inherited by American epic novels of the twentieth century. Since *Paradise Lost*, the epic in Western literature has made the exploits of the hero more spiritual than physical; instead of the prowess of his arms the progress of his soul came to matter. The transcendental poet Jones Very expressed a popular nineteenth-century view, in a well-known essay, "Epic Poetry," when he wrote that the difficulty of producing an epic in modern times is itself "proof of the progress of the soul, and of its approach to that state of being where its thought is action, its word power." [19] Had Very been able to see the full text of Wordsworth's *The Prelude*, he probably would have agreed with the growing number of contemporary readers who regard that poem as an "important mutation which adapts the epic tradition to a new spiritual or historic environment." [20] *Moby-Dick*, however, he could not have considered as anything but an unfortunate step backward, for it is the epic of the oldest tradition, the so-called primary or primitive epic, that Melville chose to imitate. His cultivated archaism is to be found in the objective of the hero's quest, a savage revenge upon a monster of the deep, in the poetic speaking style of a bard addressing an audience, and in the episodic form of the action. In the spiritualization of the epic which Very and Wordsworth critics acclaim, mental activity becomes the substance of the narrative and physical action is scanted. Alongside of *The Prelude*, in this respect, it would not be unreasonable to place James's *The Ambassadors* and Bellow's *Herzog* as works in which the rawness of action is dissolved in thought. The dominant tendency in the American epic novel, however, is the deliberate return to primitive motifs: the prowess of warriors in Cooper and Simms, the revenge against a monster in *Moby-Dick*, the battle to the death in *The Octopus* and *For Whom the Bell Tolls*, the migration of a people in *The Grapes of Wrath*. No American epic hero fights to save a city, as is so common in the Renaissance epic, but always to preserve some less sophisticated way of life.

Moby-Dick is a unique hybrid standing in no single literary tradition. Neither wholly novel nor wholly epic, it points nonetheless to the ultimate merging of the two forms in later works, for it was to be the novel, not heroic verse nor prose romance, that best inherited the function of the epic. Beginning as a parody of epic heroism and placing a high value on the accumulation

of realistic details so little in accord with the supernatural tone of the epic, the novel hardly seemed at
first to be in any way related to the epic. But as the
novel developed and dissociated itself from the romance,
it showed a remarkable capacity to assimilate the materials and forms of other genres without being harmed
by their weaknesses. The epic has been one of the
principal forms assimilated by the novel. Carlyle antici-
pated the process quite early, when he observed in 1832
that after the *Aeneid* epics grew "hollower" because the
"authentically supernatural" became mere machinery
and belief failed. "We have then, in place of the wholly
dead modern Epic, the partially living modern Novel;
to which latter it is much easier to lend that above
mentioned so essential 'momentary credence' . . . the
former being flatly incredible." [21] The novel, it would
seem, has the opportunity to do what other adaptations
of the epic had failed to do: restore to the epic tradition
what Carlyle calls the "entire credibility" (credibility
even of the supernatural) that accounts for the sur-
passing power of the early epics.

The epic tradition and the novel have been of mutual
benefit, the deficiencies of the one being corrected by the
virtues of the other. Being committed to prose of an
informal sort, the novel cannot affect the poetic conventions that led to so much of the swelling and
bombast of the Renaissance and Augustan versions of
the epic. Melville in *Moby-Dick* and James Joyce in
Ulysses go as far as it is safe to go in the direction of
poeticizing the prose of fiction, and their example, it is
worth citing as proof of the health of the novel tradition,
has not led to extravagant imitations among their successors. It is perhaps the imitation of the minutiae of
poetic conventions that has done the epic tradition most
harm; the larger features of narrative structure and tone
are more safely bequeathed, and it is these that the novel

is better disposed to borrow than any other genre. From the epic the novel inherits the simple and strong narrative framework on which to base its immense accumulation of details. The broad archetypal patterns of the hero's career and the rather solemn presentation of serious themes characteristic of the epic are given fresh life in a form that insists upon bringing into literature the factual and the existential. On the other hand, in assuming the elevated tone of the epic, the novel saves from triviality its multitudinous details. Gide's novelist in *The Counterfeiters*, Edouard, declares, "The form that tempts me is the epic. The epic tone alone suits me and has the power to satisfy me; it alone can free the novel from its realistic rut." [22] The rut may be spiritual as well as technical. In order to write a novel having "all the bright magic of the fairy tale," Ralph Ellison confessed that he was "forced to conceive of a novel unburdened by the narrow naturalism which has led after so many triumphs to the final and unrelieved despair which marks so much of our current fiction." [23]

To summarize the happy association of epic and novel: The tendency of epic writing to become bombastic is corrected by the novel's commitment to plain prose, while the triviality of the novel's facts is relieved by the epic's elevated tone. The tendency of the novel to formlessness is corrected by the epic's simple narrative unity and archetypal patterns of characterization. The antiquarianism of the epic is relieved by the contemporaneity of the novel's subject matter, and the inevitable pull of naturalism toward despair is corrected by the epic's assertion of nobility in man.

Carlyle's statement refers in general to the fact that the novel as a genre is the inheritor of the epic tradition. Some novels, it may be shown, bear a more specific relation to the epic than others. *Henry Esmond* is one such epic novel according to the careful demonstration of John Loofbourow, who describes it as "the first effective response to the critical demands for novels that would count intellectually in the same way as history, imaginatively as epic, and emotionally as a representation of the subjective truths that had become a reality for the nineteenth century." [24] Thackeray is credited with showing writers how the scope of a novel may be enlarged by fusing biographical and historical materials with epic patterns; the result is "a novel that will fulfill the epic function—epic not in an impressionistic but in a definable sense." [25]

Somewhere between the detailed requirements of a LeBossu and the loose designation of the oversize novel as epic there must be a useful definition of epic writing, if not of the epic work, from earliest times to the present. The long history of the genre makes simplification more desirable than complication in such a definition. Our first simplification must be that there are two prime epic subjects and forms: 1] the battle epic, in which many people are involved in a great action and of which the *Iliad* is the ancient and *War and Peace* the modern type, and 2] the quest epic, in which the exploits of a single hero are the subject and of which the *Odyssey* is the ancient and *Ulysses* the modern type. The form of the battle epic is governed by the principle of antithesis, or the conflict of opposed interests; the form of the quest epic is serial, or the sequence of adventures through which the hero makes his way. Our second simplification is that the epic is always marked by aggrandizement, or the imparting of consequence and gravity to action, character, and theme. Transcendence, or the endowing of human activities with wonder and mystery is one method of aggrandizement looking towards sublimity; another method, inspired by more practical ends, is didacticism, or the exemplification of estimable actions and thoughts.

Aggrandizement of action in a battle epic is achieved by the participation of a multitude of people in an event of great national or world importance. The conception of what is important is subject to change: in one age it may be rescuing a runaway wife, in another rescuing the shrine of a god. The Trojan War may have been a foolish affair, as the old men in the chorus of *Agamemnon* firmly believe, but war, for which it is a synecdoche, is not, and Homer's account of men at war is not. The subject of the epic may be pure invention, but it must appear to be part of an actual historical event, for it is this association that helps to dignify and magnify it. The public as well as the historical quality of the action contributes to the sense of its greatness. Turned outward instead of inward, human behavior in the epic is predominantly social. People freely communicate with each other and combine in innumerable ways to make a compact world of communal action and fellow feeling. Eighteenth-century criticism saw in such outwardness of behavior the result of the epic poet's imitating a primitive society, and a critic as recent as Lukács maintains that epic "can retain its public character only at a very primitive stage of social development." [26] It is perhaps in response to this ancient aspect of epic that modern epics often choose to represent a primitive group existing as an island within the civilized world, such as the Okies of *The Grapes of Wrath*, the Spanish guerillas of *For Whom the Bell Tolls*, and the Africans of *Henderson the Rain King*. Social relationships can thus be simplified in order to present more clearly the salient aims and needs of the major society.

Great length and episodic structure are the price the epic pays for proposing to treat many characters engaged in a social action over a long period of time in many different places—a price, Aristotle thought, making epic inferior to tragedy. Comprehensive and encyclopedic in its myriad details, the epic is given form, nonetheless, by virtue of the powerful attraction of its central action, what Lascelles Abercrombie calls the "relentless onward movement" of the epic, its "austere driving-forward." [27] Clearly visible against the background of innumerable details, the central action has a simple strong line of development towards a definite resolution; it remains simple by virtue of the dramatic motif of battle or conflict, which leads directly to catastrophe and to victory or loss. Epic writing is at bottom monolithic narrative of grave public import. Helping to keep the action central and forceful is the powerful visual and spatial properties of the principal action, what Thomas Greene has called the "arch-image" and Tillyard the "geographical intensity" of epic.[28] Large gestures, striking physical properties, and simple settings are vivid and eloquent supporters of the action and the meanings it conveys.

Aggrandizement of theme in the epic is accomplished by the treatment of universal concerns and the expression of widely held values. E. M. W. Tillyard calls this the "choric" element in the epic because it presents the "accepted unconscious metaphysic" of a time; Susanne Langer gets at it through the function of epic as the "apotheosis of myth," myth being the "serious envisagement of . . . fundamental truths" of the world.[29] It is not the discovery of new truths that the epic claims, but the application of old truths to newly arisen problems in the human situation. Discovery plays its part in the recognition of the appropriateness of such applications, and it is at this point that the epic becomes didactic. The motif of the hero starting out as an outsider, a sulker hugging his own selfish needs, or an apprentice to another hero, is used as a didactic strategy whereby the reader is enabled to move with the hero from ignorance to knowledge of what is expected of him.

The hero is the principal expression of the aggrandizement of character in the battle epic. Of course, all of the
figures in an epic, both small and great, are displayed as
the noblest specimens of humanity, at every level. But
no one shares the hero's eminence, his exceptional
capacity for action, self-determination, and the expen-
diture of great energy in a cause that does not serve his
self-interest. The hero begins as an outsider who grows
in awareness of a human crisis and is gradually drawn
into a cause calculated to cope with it. His is not an
accidental involvement but the result of a systematic
consecration: the obligation to a companion who has
gone before, the influence of a brotherhood of warriors,
the benediction of divinities, the privileged descent
into the underworld where his heroic character is
strengthened and a new life granted.

The hero is the least stable element in the tradition
of the epic. What remains intact is honor, or the need
the hero feels to stake his interests and his life in a great
enterprise with other men. This he freely chooses to do,
and so chooses death. What has changed is the extent
of the hero's participation in great affairs; the modern
hero is no longer cast as an outstanding leader with
extraordinary abilities, and if he has innate virtue it is
his common heritage as man rather than the sign of
exceptional origin. Achilles and Aeneas may be en-
trapped to perform noble deeds, but they are able to
project their heroic choices against a noble background
and the certain expectation of the world, their fame
going before them, whereas the modern hero has only
his representative common humanity to spring from.
This is particularly the case in the novel, a genre in
which character is drawn more nearly from the experience of the author than modeled upon some figure
already active in the imagination of his readers. The
novelist's here is no longer the legendary figure seen from

a distance that lends magnitude but rather a reflection of the novelist himself placed experimentally upon a great national stage. He has considerably more inwardness than his earlier counterparts, and his inwardness involves questioning the value of heroism itself. The hero of the American epic novel is an apprentice-hero, rather like Telemachus than Roland, who has latent heroic energy and must learn the cause he is willing to serve and the manner in which he must serve it. Often he ends his career in the novel as a man prepared to act heroically rather than one who has acted heroically. Far from damaging the concept of heroism, the democratization of the epic hero's attributes in some ways makes heroic action in the present more demanding and more defiant of the fate that restricts the ambition of men. In whatever degree, the participation of the hero in the principal action is required and his fulfillment as an individual must be accomplished in terms of the principal action.

Aggrandizement in the Odyssean quest epic is expressed by material dealing with the most significant crisis in the life of a representative man: his decision to live or die. From a condition in his life leading him from frustration to despair, and possibly to suicide, the hero embarks upon a search for something worth living for and worth doing. Often this is found in an ultimate return to his origins, to an activity that preceded his troubled times, or to a role in which he finds new reason to be proud. On the isle of Ogygia, Odysseus, deprived of his rightful place and name in Ithaca, and subjected to the wrath of an antagonistic god, contemplates suicide; the perilous journey home and the fight against his enemies bring an end to the despair of namelessness by restoring him to his proper identity as a king in the land where he is known. He reaches this end only after a series of tests in which he must conceal his identity and then reveal it until he discovers the man he truly is. The adventures on his homeward voyage are either obstructions blocking his progress or instructions preparing him for future trials. The obstructive adventures are terrors that paralyze (Polyphemus) and temptations that threaten to divert (Sirens). The hero must find his way between the loss of senses and their excessive gratification. Especially important as an instructive adventure is the experience of death, or the vision of death, from which the wanderer receives knowledge essential to the completion of his quest.

The function of the underworld trip develops in the history of the epic from the direct warnings Odysseus receives in Hades, through the elaborate pattern of instruction and homily in Dante, to the symbolical representation of death and rebirth of the hero in the modern treatments of the motif. Instead of going simply to consult the dead, the modern hero descends into the underworld to slough off an inefficacious identity and assume a new heroic role; the new knowledge he receives is his recognition of new life possibilities. The descent, for both ancient and modern heroes, is a special mark of distinction. "One death is enough for most men," Circe says to Odysseus after his return from Hades, "but you will now have two." The descent into the underworld and the intervention of divinities in his life are the two principal consecrations of the exceptional man. The experience of death is typical of the wondrous and privileged quality of the epic hero's exploits; he may return to a world of a very real sort, the kingdom of Ithaca, but his adventures on the road are fabulous. Yet it is from the fabulous experiences that the hero learns things that cannot be learned from ordinary circumstances, and it is the fabulous experience that prepares him for contending with reality. To the depth psychologist this is another way of saying that in the world of his dreams and subconscious mind the individual has revealed to him much that escapes him in his waking life and can be turned to account.

If the battle epic pictures the gathering of community forces to combat some enemy or condition threatening the existence of all, the quest epic is the gathering of an individual's forces in the search of a meaning for his life, a reason not to give up life. While the great lesson of the battle epic is that no man stands alone, being alone and cut off from others is the starting condition of the quest epic. Eventually, however, the completion of a successful quest leads the hero to a reintegration with the community, and we end with a principle which is taken for granted in the battle epic.

As the more commodious form, the battle epic can incorporate elements of and sometimes, as in the *Aeneid,* the whole of a quest epic. The much simpler form of the quest epic is derived from the seriality of its material in which one adventure follows discretely upon another in a repetitive, rather than complicated pattern. The strict linearity of the episodes is relieved by two devices: circularity, or bringing the hero in his last adventure to a point corresponding to his first; and *in medias res,* or starting the series somewhere in the middle and then working backward and forward. There can also be a counterpointing of the fabulous with the realistic adventures that lends contrast and variety of the sort remarked by Longinus is his comments on the *Odyssey.*

In reply to a question about the meaning of the title *Light in August,* William Faulkner said he was referring to a "peculiar quality to light" that occurs for a brief spell in his country during the month of August: a "foretaste of fall, it's cool, there's a lambence, a luminous quality to the light, as though it came not from just today but from back in the old classic times . . . from Greece, from Olympus . . . a luminosity older than our

Christian civilization." [30] We are reminded of Simms's observation that the "sky and atmosphere" of the South and ancient Greece are alike; and from New England there is a similar note in Thoreau's comment in the chapter entitled "Sunday" in *A Week on the Concord and Merrimack Rivers* that the *Iliad* "embodies still all the sunlight that fell on Asia Minor. . . . The ruins of Egypt oppress and stifle us with their dust. . . . But the rays of Greek poetry struggle down to us, and mingle with the sunbeams of the recent day." The heroine in *Light in August* with whom Faulkner associates the peculiar light of Greece is Lena Grove, a poor country girl in trouble and yet a kind of earth goddess living in perfect harmony with the cycles of day and night, birth and death. A creature of her time and place, yet unperturbed by them, fixed and yet always moving (in pursuit of her lover), she is like a figure on Keats's Grecian urn: "backrolling now behind her a long monotonous succession of peaceful and undeviating changes from day to dark and dark to day again, through which she advanced in identical and anonymous and deliberate wagons as though through a succession of creakwheeled and limpeared avatars, like something moving forever and without progress across an urn." [31] What Faulkner so successfully captures in this first chapter of *Light in August* is the effect of temporal and spatial expansiveness, an imaginable infinity, so to speak, in which the commonest experiences, like riding a wagon on country roads, become weighty, awesome, fabulous. Melville often achieves the same effect in *Moby-Dick*, and Thomas Wolfe attempts to render what he calls the "one moment of timeless suspension." Wolfe, like Faulkner, associates this moment with a certain quality of light, "old and tragic," that fixes George Webber in a magic moment, "something like old time and destiny." [32] The bringing together of the past and the present, the far and the near, has much to do with this effect as do style and the use of mythic material, or what in the traditional epic would be identified by criticism as elevated language and the intervention of the gods. By far the most important ingredient of epic writing, style, and myth are tools of aggrandizement creating transcendent tone. A work having explicit and detailed parallels to the *Odyssey* of Homer, such as Gerald Sykes's *The Center of the Stage* (1952), for example, falls short of the ultimate epic distinction because its tone remains naturalistic throughout, while Hemingway's *The Old Man and the Sea*, a brief work without specific epic conventions, has in great degree the epic quality of large symbolic power and transcendent tone.

Inheriting the epic, the novel necessarily inherits myth, which is crystallized and transmitted by epic writing. Myth in turn contributes to the novel transcendent tone and a supply of narrative motifs, especially motifs associated with the exploits of the hero. Because it is a prose narrative of a realistic kind, the novel is necessarily limited in the degree to which it can employ elevated language and myth. To be made acceptable in a novel myth must undergo what Northrop Frye calls "displacement," a process in which some of the force of myth is lost in being transformed into the "incidental, even coincidental or accidental, imagery" of the realistic novel.[33] Similarly, the novelist's effort to attain elevation of style is severely limited by the nature of prose itself. But there are advantages accruing from the limitations imposed by adaptive techniques. The excesses of elevated style are more readily avoided in prose than in verse adaptations of the epic manner, and the association of myth with the details of ordinary contemporary existence mitigates the bald phantasy of myth and makes it viable to the modern reader.

2

The Octopus

Of all the writers with whom we have to deal, Frank Norris was the most ambitious to produce a novel in the epic tradition. Following the example of Zola, he thought of the novel as the epic of the present age, and, in an article entitled "A Neglected Epic," urged American authors to write about the winning of the West as "the last great epic event in the history of civilization" worthy of comparison with the events that were celebrated in the *Odyssey* and the *Song of Roland.*[1] He was modest enough not to cite his own book, *The Octopus,* as having already treated a part of that epic subject, although while he was working on the book he did not hesitate to describe it to his friends, including William Dean Howells, as "a big epic trilogy," a "big, epic, dramatic thing."[2] The first edition proudly bore the subtitle "The Epic of Wheat." From Howells to Granville Hicks friendly critics have accepted Norris's denomination of his work. In one review Howells called the book a "prodigious epic," in another a social epic standing as an *Iliad* in relation to *McTeague*, which he deemed an *Odyssey* or "personal epic."[3] Hicks has said that *The Octopus* is "not wholly unworthy of the name of epic"; Parrington, that it is an "epic of the soil."[4]

The Octopus is the epic novel that Frank Norris went on to write, so to speak, after Presley, the young poet in the story, gave up his project to write a poem worthy of Homer, whose *Odyssey* he carried in his pocket in a "little tree-calf edition." Presley's design for "the great poem of the West" is carefully proved to be false because of its romantic materials: reminiscences of the original Spanish grandees in the West, the "strange history" of an Indian's tragic love affair, and a Mission church which the poet prized as "a note of the Old World"—all this to be done in thundering hexameters. All thought of his marvelous poem is driven from his mind, however, when Presley witnesses a horrible accident in which a railroad engine charges into a flock of sheep that had strayed onto the track. Had he not been such a slave to the romantic tradition in literature, the poet would have found his epic subject in what that accident symbolized: the desperate economic struggle between the monopoly power of the railroad trust and the helpless ranchers of the San Joaquin Valley. "Pres, my boy, there is your epic poem ready to hand," he is later told by an astute manufacturer. But Presley cannot see this at the time, for he must begin his career as a poet all over again and learn to respect the hard facts of the life of the people and the region he wanted to write about. Instead of doing an epic on "the forerunners of empire" in the West, he writes a short poem, "The Toilers," expressing his indignation over the exploitation of the People. From epic poet he has descended to social protester.

Norris is presumably an older and wiser Presley who has discovered the form that the epic must take when it is modified by the techniques of naturalism. His subject is not strictly one of "the various fightings westward" recommended in "A Neglected Epic," but rather the economic war between impersonal monopoly and small entrepreneurs for the control of wheat production after the land has been settled. Norris's particular example of this worldwide conflict happens to be drawn from the

history of California; it could have occurred almost
anywhere in the world, but it is the Western setting and
the Western scale of things that supplied Norris with the
details of vast size, number, and space that give the
work what Howells identified as its "Homeric largeness."

The scope of the action is clear as we are introduced
to the predicament of hundreds of people—ranchers,
their families, and employees—who are fighting to save
their property and livelihood from the forces of the railroad—its owners, agents, and supporting lawmen. The
ranchers (actually wheat farmers) have farms of about
ten thousand acres each; the railroad alone owns a mil-
lion acres, "infinite, illimitable, stretching out there
under the sheen of the sunset forever and forever." [5]
Always Norris keeps before the reader the image of limit-
less land, the wheat growing on the land, and the gigantic working of the land by men. In one farming opera-
tion thirty-five ploughs, "each drawn by its team of
ten, stretched in an interminable line, nearly a quarter
of a mile in length." The land is the novel's arch-image,
inspiring awe and at the same time constituting both
the scene and the prize of a desperate struggle among
men. Norris's descriptions of the land and the growing
wheat, his accounts of mass ploughing, planting, and
harvesting are his principal means of striking the epic
note of the fabulous and the wonderful. His ultimate
reach for this kind of tone is seen in his repeated metaphor of the land as a goddess, a Titan "offering herself
to the caress of the plough" and being satisfied by men
who accomplish their worship by making her productive. The sexual act is never detailed by Norris except
in relation to massive agricultural processes; we are told
about thirty-three grain drills "seeding the ten thousand
acres of the great ranch; fecundating the living soil;
implanting deep in the dark womb of the Earth the
germ of life, the sustenance of a whole world, the food

of an entire People" (p. 122). Norris's epic is about gods as well as men, about the primordial forces that bind men, in whatever time, to life, hunger, death, and reproduction.

The numerous characters in *The Octopus* are only a little less aggrandized than the lordly land they inhabit. Norris is particularly fond of the "epic simplicity and directness" of these people and brings them together in large groups for "Homeric" feasts, games, and entertainments. This glorification of the People (always capitalized) is a product not only of Norris's fervid Anglo-Saxonism but of the widespread notion, dating from eighteenth-century criticism, that ordinary characters in epic literature were actually modeled after the honest and sturdy folk of primitive societies. We find the same notion of the heroic folk in Steinbeck's Okies and, without the Anglo-Saxonism, in Hemingway's Spanish peasants. In *The Octopus*, part of the effect of aggrandizement is secured by describing the participation of the People in ceremonial rituals, such as the dedication of a new barn or the yearly round-up and killing of jack-rabbits, accounted "an epic in brief" by one critic.[6]

In addition to making frequent allusions to Homer and the *Odyssey*, Norris uses Homeric epithets consistently with certain characters: Hilma always has "thick moist hair," Angéle "lips of almost Egyptian fullness." Almost every time reference is made to the love affair of Angéle and Vanamee, the place in which they meet, the prowler who comes between them, and the two lovers themselves are described in paragraphs that are practically identical except for slight changes in phrasing. Hamlin Garland compared these devices to the leit-motif in Wagnerian opera, and Howells, who first called attention to the epic qualities of *The Octopus*, somehow missed their origin and regarded them as a mere "trick" in characterization.[7]

There is considerably less straining after epic tags in

Norris's treatment of the conflict between the railroad and the ranchers. The violence and manners of the West gave him a ready source of details for the machinery of warfare so essential in a battle epic. The economic conflict, which is the basis of the whole book, is transformed from a matter of contracts, prices, and property rights to a very exciting account of armed might and strategies, of councils of war and the rivalry of leaders, of alliances and betrayals. Although the moves of the enemy, the monopoly power, are properly shrouded in mystery—as they are in *The Grapes of Wrath*—we get a close view of the ranchers in their efforts to survive. At their many councils there is much vociferous argument as they debate the steps to be taken in the war against the railroad. Each of the ranchers is a powerful, baronial chieftain figure ruling over domains as large as those of minor kings. Osterman, one of the ranchers, is the Thersites of these sessions:

> Osterman got on his feet; leaning across the table, gesturing wildly with his right hand, his serio-comic face, with its bald forehead and stiff red ears, was inflamed with excitement. He took the floor, creating an impression, attracting all attention to himself, playing to the gallery, gesticulating, clamourous, full of noise. (P. 76)

The Achilles who collides with him is Annixter, another rancher, while Magnus Derrick, who is appointed by the ranchers to be their leader, is a kind of Agamemnon.

The best developed character in the book, Annixter goes through a process of radical change of the same sort that Achilles underwent. We see him first as a comic figure, prone to anger of a peevish sort. Before the first council meeting is over he withdraws his support from the cause and is persuaded to rejoin his fellows only "after interminable argument." Why did he sulk? Because a practical joker had put "sloop" (pudding sauce) in his bed. The high point of his early career is a gun duel which is staged rather grandly as a formal confrontation of warriors before an assembled populace. Annixter gets his man, an aggrieved cow "buster," but he is not quite sure how he came out alive: "He was overwhelmed with astonishment. Why, after the shooting began he had not so much as seen Delaney with any degree of plainness. The whole affair was a whirl." Although Norris does not miss the chance for some exciting action, there is something slightly ridiculous about the encounter and the manner in which Annixter receives the plaudits of the assembled women: "He delivered himself of a remembered phrase, very elegant, refined. It was Lancelot after the tournament, Bayard receiving felicitations after the battle."

Annixter is moved by anger. It was "mere love of contention" that made him commit himself to the ranchers' cause in the first place, and in council he argues for war against the railroad simply because his contentiousness forces him to oppose the viewpoint of Magnus Derrick, a prominent rancher who is reluctant to do battle with the railroad. In the early stages of the struggle, he never displays more than a superficial awareness of the seriousness of the whole affair and his part in it. He shows himself to be self-centered, hypochondriacal, and surly. Only Presley can contradict him without his "picking a quarrel upon the instant." It is not the love of a friend that brings this Achilles around, however; the anger in Annixter is snapped by his realization of love for a woman, Hilma Tree, and from that point on his character undergoes a radical change. It is typical of the imagery of the book that his love grows in him and then suddenly bursts like a seed:

Annixter stood suddenly upright, a mighty tenderness, a gentleness of spirit, such as he had never conceived of, in his heart strained, swelled, and in a moment seemed to burst. Out of the dark furrows of his soul, up from the deep rugged recesses of his being, something rose, expanding. (P. 252)

Married happily to Hilma, Annixter begins to develop a concern for all people and even reaches out to help those who have been hurt by the war with the railroad. Annixter begins his career as a comic figure in the familiar Western story of the uncouth male's awakening to feminine influence; in the end he appears as a man of truly heroic proportions. His consecration to others reads very much like that of a later American hero, Tom Joad in *The Grapes of Wrath*:

And I began to see that a fellow can't live *for* himself any more than he can live *by* himself. He's got to think of others. If he's got brains, he's got to think for the poor ducks that haven't 'em, and not give 'em a boot in the backsides because they happen to be stupid; and if he's got money, he's got to help those that are busted, and if he's got a house, he's got to think of those that ain't got anywhere to go. I've got a whole lot of ideas since I began to love Hilma, and just as soon as I can, I'm going to get in and *help* people, and I'm going to keep to that idea the rest of my natural life. That ain't much of a religion, but it's the best I've got, and Henry Ward Beecher couldn't do any more than that. (P. 321)

Just as in Tom's thinking, service to humanity becomes here a substitute for religion. Annixter's anger, his "fierce truculency," like Achilles', is transformed into compassion; but before anything can be made of his new life, he dies in a skirmish with the supporters of the railroad, ironically as he is trying to play the role of a peacemaker.

While Annixter lends himself to Norris's development of a humorous frontier hero, there can be no question that Magnus Derrick is conceived in the tradition of
the tragic hero as king and patriarch. He is acclaimed
by all as the natural leader of the ranchers, who saw in
his manner "something Jovian," and trembled when
he was angry. His ambition is to exercise power, to be
the master of men; and his ambition soars even beyond the state of California to dreams of empire: "He
saw his wheat, like the crest of an advancing billow,
crossing the Pacific, bursting upon Asia, flooding the
Orient in a golden torrent." So great is his ambition
that Derrick risks his reputation by yielding to the
ranchers' demands to proceed against the railroad by
underhanded means. This leads to "his fall, his ruin";
he is betrayed both by his son Lyman, who sells out to
the enemy, and by the man he has paid to keep his
questionable practices secret. The career of Magnus
Derrick comes to a tragic end—"deserted by his friends,
his son murdered, his dishonesty known, an old man,
broken, discarded, discredited, and abandoned."

Derrick is the hero as king, an Agamemnon figure,
and his portrait is heroic in every respect except his
language. He is reputed to be "one of the last of the followers of the old school of orators," but we get no
evidence of this in his speeches at the many councils he
presides over. Norris's inability to endow him with
speech worthy of his heroic role seriously hurts the
characterization of Magnus Derrick. The extent of his
failure can be measured by the success of a character
similarly conceived, Captain Ahab. Another kingly hero,
Ahab is also engaged in mortal and hopeless combat with
a monster that has hurt him, but he is a much more
effective figure because of the "bold and nervous lofty
language" that Melville was able to fashion for his
great speeches. Both Derrick and Ahab are tragic heroes

in that the interest in them is contained within the circle of their personal predicaments and does not expand into the social contexts around them. Their origin in the dramatic genre remains visible: Ahab has precious little existence apart from his own speeches and the speeches of other characters about him; while Derrick has a more novelistic presence, he is shown off best at the councils of the embattled wheat-growers. The scene in which his leadership is brutally challenged takes place in an Opera House, and his defeat is confirmed immediately afterwards in the dressing room of "the leading actress of a comic-opera troupe." He lives on in senile and abject servility to the powers that he had set out to overthrow. In Annixter, Norris is submitting heroism to the test of ridicule, in Derrick to the test of tragedy.

The shepherd Vanamee is Norris's third version of the hero. His story is just the kind that the poet Presley had in mind to write before he was thrust into the world of contemporary events. Its action is mystical and vague, its scene a "little cloister garden" of an old Mission, "shut off, discreet, romantic, a garden of dreams, of enchantments, of illusions." To this "corner of romance" Vanamee comes to seek his sweetheart, Angéle Varian, who died in childbirth within a year after a "prowler of the night" had raped her. After the tragedy Vanamee disappeared and wandered for eighteen years over the Southwest, spending two years as a recluse in the desert of Arizona. Upon his return the vision of Angéle appears to him hovering in the moonlight over the blossoming acres of an abandoned seed farm that had once been cultivated by the girl's parents. Actually, the "vision" is the daughter of Angéle, whom Vanamee has succeeded in rousing from her sleep by the power he has of calling people to him by psychic suggestion alone. The story of Vanamee and Angéle supplies Norris with the stuff of the wondrous and fabulous characteristic of epic narrative. Although nothing supernatural actually occurs, Norris treats the romance in such a way that Vanamee's experience is passed off as miraculous, while the natural explanation is kept waiting and is, at best, obscure. Both the transcendence of epic and the verisimilitude required by the novel are thus satisfied.

Vanamee is Norris's Orpheus seeking his departed lover, who, like Eurydice, has been ravished by a "serpent . . . that prowler of the night, that strange fearful figure with the unseen face, swooping in there from out the darkness, gone in an instant, yet leaving behind the trail and trace of death and of pollution." Vanamee's midnight vigils in the Mission garden, where there are nine graves, including Angéle's, are his descent into the land of the dead to rescue his beloved with the help of his magical gift of thought transference. In accordance with the Orpheus myth Norris describes him as a "poet by instinct," a gentle and reserved shepherd, a lover of the sky. He is distraught over the loss of his sweetheart and night after night he exerts his "curious power of attraction" in order to call Angéle back from the grave. "Come to me—Angéle—don't you hear? Come to me," pleads Vanamee, whose name is perhaps derived from the Mexican-Spanish *vén(g)e me* (come to me). Not until the spring of the year is his cry answered, when "his outstretched hands, groping in the darkness, met the touch of other fingers." It is Angéle:

> From out this life of flowers, this world of colour, this atmosphere oppressive with perfume, this darkness clogged and cloyed, and thickened with sweet odours, she came to him. She came to him from out of the flowers, the smell of the roses in her hair of gold, the aroma and the imperial red of the carnations

in her lips, the whiteness of the lilies, the perfume of the lilies, and the lilies' slender, balancing grace in her neck. Her hands disengaged the scent of the heliotrope. The folds of her scarlet gown gave off the enervating smell of poppies. Her feet were redolent of hyacinth. (P. 268)

The flowers are actually growing on the old seed farm in the valley where Angéle's daughter is walking in her sleep, but to Vanamee the flowers are in Hades and his former sweetheart is the prisoner of Death.[8] But Death has not destroyed her beauty, for in the "Vision" she appears in all the glory of her youth and "deathless beauty." Finally, at the time of the wheat harvest, the "Vision" becomes a reality—"Angéle in the flesh, vital, sane, material." She comes "from the entrance of the little valley" and stands "realized in the wheat" and in the sunlight. Vanamee rushes to embrace her.

Vanamee's acceptance of Angéle's daughter as essentially Angéle herself indicates his belief in the transmigration of souls, one of the three principal doctrines of Orphism. The association of Vanamee with the sky and Angéle with the cycle of life and death is in accord with ancient myth. Eurydice, writes Jane Harrison, "is . . . but the ordered form of Earth herself in her cyclic movement of life and death." [9] This leads us to another myth which Norris employs in order to relate the story of his lovers to the theme of his novel. The maiden dwelling in the realm of death, the imagery of queenliness, the profusion of flowers in every description of the "Vision," and particularly the association of growing wheat with the return of the departed daughter to life point to the myth of Demeter and Persephone. To Vanamee, Angéle and her daughter appear as a single person; even when the daughter is finally distinguished from the mother in order to preserve realism,

Vanamee rejects the distinction: "Angéle or Angéle's daughter, it was all one with him." This accords in the myth with the merging of the goddesses into a single figure, which is noted both by anthropologists, who speak of "the essential identity of mother and daughter," and by Jungian psychologists, who interpret Demeter and Persephone as a single anima capable of self-renewal.[10] The goddess Hecate, who witnessed the rape of Persephone (according to the Homeric "Hymn to Demeter"), is represented by the prominence given to the moon in Norris's descriptions of the "Vision." It is at "the rising of the full moon" that Vanamee always sees the awful phenomenon: "The moon had risen. Its great shield stood over the eastern horizon. Within six feet of Vanamee, clear and distinct, against the disk of the moon, stood the figure of a young girl." Norris's use of the moon is precisely in the sense in which C. Kerenyi sees the ambiguous role of Hecate in the Demeter world: "on the one hand we have motherly solicitude and the growth of all living things, on the other more indecency and deadliness." [11] Angéle's final appearance, when Vanamee has his triumph, occurs in "the blinding light of the day" when she is no longer "an hallucination of the moonlight." [12]

To underscore the life-cycle theme Norris mingles Christian scripture with pagan myth. Vanamee is repeatedly associated with "the inspired shepherds of the Hebraic legends, living close to nature, the younger prophets of Israel, dwellers in the wilderness, solitary, imaginative, believing in the Vision, having strange delusions, gifted with strange powers." From Father Sarria, the Catholic priest of the Mission church, he first hears the words from St. Paul: "How are the dead raised up? And with what body do they come? Thou fool! That which thou sowest is not quickened except it die." In his grief over the loss of Angéle, Vanamee cannot ap-

preciate this truth even though Father Sarria tries to
strengthen his point by making an analogy with the
growing of wheat: "Your grain of wheat is your symbol
of immortality. You bury it in the earth. It dies, and
rises again a thousand times more beautiful. Vanamee,
your dear girl was only a grain of humanity that we
have buried here, and the end is not yet." The priest
adds significantly: "But all this is so old, so old. The
world learned it a thousand years ago, and yet each man
that has ever stood by the open grave of anyone he
loved must learn it all over again from the beginning."
It is, of course, as old as the myth of Demeter and
Persephone in which, according to Frazer, Demeter is
the "seed-corn of last year" and Persephone the ripe
ear of this year, or as old as the ritual of the Cherokee
Indians who lamented the bloody death of the Old
Woman of the Corn from whose blood the new corn
springs.[13] Whether he drew from Frazer, whose *Golden
Bough* appeared in 1890, or from firsthand knowledge
of the rituals of American Indians, we may never know,
but Norris evidently appreciated such material and saw
clearly the relation of primitive harvest rites to the
Christian idea of resurrection. Significantly, it is Vanamee—"tanned as an Indian, lean as an Indian, with an
Indian's long black hair"—who witnesses these ancient
mysteries; it is Vanamee who identifies the sprouting
wheat with the resurrection of Angéle in the person of
her daughter. Christianity merely confirms a truth that
Vanamee learns more directly from "a modern Proser-
pina" who teaches him "that nothing dies." [14]

Norris's third interesting young man, Presley, is more
complex than Annixter and Vanamee because he represents the young Norris himself with all his ambiguities
subjectively treated, whereas Annixter and Vanamee
are expressions of single aspects of Norris's personality magnified and more or less objectively viewed from

a distance. Presley is not only a candidate for heroic honors to be gained by performing great deeds, he is also a prospective Homer celebrating those deeds in epic song. His is an apprenticeship in letters as well as heroism: as a poet he must learn to surrender the romantic literary notions that he had brought with him from the East and discover a true subject for his talent to work on, the contemporary life of men; and as a hero he must find a cause worth committing himself to. Although he has only one short poem, "The Toilers," to show for his pains, he succeeds better in the first enterprise than in the second, for even though his eyes are finally opened to the justice of the ranchers' cause and to the evil of the railroad, his commitment comes too late to do any good. He finds a cause but cannot develop the means to serve it. He has the young man's vague ambition to be a hero, "a vast desire to acquit himself of some terrible deed of readjustment, just what, he could not say, some terrifying martyrdom, some awe-inspiring immolation, consummate, incisive, conclusive," but he does not have the energy and will to devote himself steadily to the work of a hero, for "his constitutional irresoluteness obstructed his path continually; brain-sick, weak of will, emotional, timid even, he temporized, procrastinated, brooded; came to decisions in the dark hours of the night, only to abandon them in the morning." Eventually, he performs two acts, delivering an impassioned speech to the League and attempting to assassinate S. Behrman, the railroad's agent and chief enemy visible to the ranchers. Both gestures are inspired by his conversations with Caraher, an anarchist, and both fail. In its doctrinaire political radicalism the speech is beyond the comprehension of the ranchers with their limited objectives, and the bomb he tosses into Behrman's house misses the mark.

Even had these extreme measures succeeded, Pres-

ley's failure would have been complete, for he finally
comes to the realization that the violence advocated by
anarchist theory is no answer to the ranchers' problem.
There is, indeed, no act of any man that can help
them, their struggles being as nothing in the face of the
power that governs life: "Force only existed—Force
that brought men into the world, Force that drowded
them out of it to make way for the succeeding generation. . . ." (p. 436). This is, of course, Norris's naturalism speaking out, with the same effect here as the
idea of fate in the classical epic. Presley seizes this "explanation of existence" only "for one instant," and in
this fleeting awareness of a force that makes a mockery
of man's heroism he is very much in the tradition of
epic heroes like Achilles and Hector. He is different, however, in his failure to return to heroic action, as they do,
in spite of their tragic recognition. Presley's battle experience crushes him, and his spirit does not revive, although it is suggested that a journey to the East (India)
and the influence of a kore-maiden will someday bring
him around, but not necessarily to heroism. Just before
he embarks on a ship that is taking a cargo of wheat to
India, he meets Hilma, now Annixter's widow, "a queen
in exile," and she has upon him the same effect she
had on Annixter:

> Then suddenly, all the tired heart of him went out
> toward her. A longing to give the best that was in
> him to the memory of her, to be strong and noble
> because of her, to reshape his purposeless, half-wasted
> life with her nobility and purity and gentleness for his
> inspiration leaped all at once within him, leaped and
> stood firm, hardening to a resolve stronger than any
> he had ever known. (P. 433)

The erotic imagery here is supported, more delicately,
in their subsequent conversation when a promise of
future love is exchanged, a possibility that after a spell

abroad he will return to become her husband, to be "very kind" to her, as she puts it in the language of genteel romance.

"Ishmael is . . . but one part of the split epic hero . . . whose other part is Ahab," declares Leslie Fiedler.[15] *The Octopus* splits the epic hero into four parts: Annixter represents his Achillean features, Derrick his tragic, Vanamee his Orphic, and Presley his contemporary. Through his close association with the other three men Presley becomes somewhat identified with their several kinds of heroism without committing himself to any. He may someday take the place of Annixter by marrying his widow, but we do not find him affirming Annixter's heroic purpose; he has pitied Derrick in his fall, but has none of his qualities of leadership; he has the knowledge of the cycle of life, but not Vanamee's miraculous encounter with it. Like Ishmael, Presley observes, from the vantage point of a literary intelligence, a variety of heroes struggling with the monster. His own role lacks commitment. Presley is Norris's literary naturalist in training who is set the task of scouting the possibilities of heroic action in economic warfare. At the end of the book he stands readier than he was at the beginning. But readier for what? To go on a journey across the sea and return to fight another day? Perhaps. At least he seems nearer to that than Ishmael and Huck.

In the notes he made for *The Octopus*, Norris called for a contrast of Hilma and Angéle on the principle that one was always to be "seen in the sun" and the other "at night under the moon."[16] The contrast was executed as planned, but the two characters turn out to be very much alike in the roles they play as maiden-goddesses bringing truth and succor to the three young heroes who stand in need of help. The deification of Angéle has already been established. That Hilma is also to be received as a goddess seems at once clear from the resplendency of her first appearance:

> Hilma stood bathed from head to foot in the torrent of sunlight that poured in upon her from the three wide-open windows. She was charming, delicious, radiant of youth, of health, of well-being. Into her eyes, wide open, brown, rimmed with their fine, thin line of intense black lashes, the sun set a diamond flash; the same golden light glowed all around her thick, moist hair, lambent, beautiful, a sheen of almost metallic lustre, and reflected itself upon her wet lips, moving with the words of her singing. The whiteness of her skin under the caress of this hale, vigorous morning light was dazzling, pure, of a fineness beyond words. Beneath the sweet modulation of her chin, the reflected light from the burnished copper vessel she was carrying set a vibration of pale gold. (P. 114)

Like Angéle, Hilma is identified by Homeric epithets; again and again we hear of her "thick, moist hair" and "large, white arms." And like Angéle she suffers an eclipse when, in the company of her parents, she retreats to the city after Annixter has made improper advances. Living in the city is a kind of death, from which she is rescued by Annixter, who offers marriage and thus restores her to "the solitary expanse of the ranches, the level reaches between the horizons, full of light and silence." Ironically, Hilma, the goddess of light and life, is served with the death of her husband and the miscarriage of her child by him, while Angéle, the goddess of death, is restored to life through her daughter. In the closing pages Hilma is seen as a tragic figure, "a queen in exile."

A third young lady is Minna Hooven, the daughter of a farmer who has been ruined by the rate-gouging practices of the railroad and later killed in the battle at the irrigation ditch. Minna is presented in the familiar naturalistic pattern of the decline of a woman from respectability and purity to poverty and vice. After Hooven's death, Minna, her mother, and baby sister go to find work in the city, San Francisco. Evicted from their lodging house for failing to pay rent, the mother and daughter are by chance separated. Frightened over losing her mother and not having a place to sleep, Minna roams the city in terror, exhausting one possibility of help after another—the church, employment, and Presley, who is at the same time looking for her. She crosses the Bay on a ferryboat and finally comes to the campus of the State University at Berkeley. A "grove of gigantic live-oaks," is the scene of Minna's "rape"; there she meets a stranger, a procuress, and at the end of a week, when Presley sees her on the street, she is a full-fledged prostitute. In response to his questions she says: "I don't know where Mamma is . . . We got separated and I never have been able to find her again. . . . Oh, I've gone to hell. It was either that or starvation" (p. 404). Her mother has starved to death, her baby sister has been saved by a wealthy woman.

Clearly another Persephone-Eurydice figure, Minna is done in the naturalistic manner, as Angéle is done in the romantic and Hilma in the tragic. Vanamee rescues Angéle from death, Annixter rescues Hilma from the city—a kind of death, and Presley, as he has failed in everything else, fails to rescue Minna from "the Terror of the City," or what in his Victorian mind he considers a fate "worse than the worst." Angéle's daughter survives and replaces her, the Hooven baby survives her mother. The mixture of naturalism and romanticism—in its mythopoeic aspect—is well illustrated by Norris's treatment of the Hooven family. The father, driven by economic forces, sacrifices his life in a conflict that starts as an epic war and ends in a fiasco; in a melodramatic sequence, the mother dies of starvation while one daughter is rescued; the other daughter "falls" in a manner reminiscent of both myth and naturalistic precedent.

In his prodigal way Norris presents in *The Octopus* four heroes, three heroines, and four literary forms. Annixter is the center of a comic plot, Magnus Derrick of a tragedy, Vanamee of a romance, and Presley of an epic including the other three actions as well as the great struggle of the ranchers and the railroad. Derrick inspires pity only. Each of the three younger heroes experiences an awakening that purifies him of some kind of anger and restores him to health and life: Annixter is purged of his surly way with people, Vanamee of his sorrow and his anger against God for allowing death in the world, and Presley of his anger over the injustices of economic process. New truths take the place of anger: Annixter learns compassion, Vanamee apprehends the cycle of life and death, and Presley discovers the law of economic determinism, or the law that looks indifferently on the good and evil of man's life. The experiences of awakening are like epiphanies for Annixter and Vanamee in that they are brought on by the sudden recognition of divine presences, Angéle and Hilma. They come at the very same time in the story and within a few pages of each other. At the close of chapter 2, book two, Annixter's bonds are broken when the realization of his love for Hilma "bursts into life within him." With "a Memnonian cry" he greets "the new-risen sun." Vanamee happens upon Annixter during his six-hour vigil but without making his presence known: "For a moment, the life-cycles of these two men, of so widely differing characters, touched each other, there in the silence of the night, under the stars." On that same morning Vanamee goes on to his own triumph, the resurrection of Angéle in the person of her daughter. In each instance the experience is followed by an apostrophe to the growing wheat; the relationship between the return of spring and rebirth is thus made perfectly clear. Presley's awakening is not inspired by woman or goddess but is the result of his groping for artistic expression. On the same night that Annixter and Vanamee are having their awakenings, Presley succeeds in completing a poem about the economic exploitation of people. Knowledge of the actual life of people in the San Joaquin Valley has led him to a victory over the romantic conception of art with which he had set out when he came to the West and has confirmed him in the writing of realistic literature. Presley's is a victory that critics like Howells, and Norris himself, wanted for the new writers of America. Artist that he is, however, Presley cannot be as certain of his victory as his friends are of theirs; as soon as the poem is finished he begins to doubt whether it is a forceful enough protest against injustice. Vanamee confirms its merit for him: "It is Truth. You have come back to the primal heart of things, and you have seen clearly." Thus Presley, though by a different route, seems to have made a discovery just as important to himself as his friends' discoveries have been to them.

From his mystical experience with the "dead," Vanamee learns truths that Presley, involved with reality, does not learn until much later. Faith in resurrection leads Vanamee away from despair to an acceptance of life, while with Presley it is the recognition of the principle of force that steels him to the tragedy of the ranchers: "Men were naught, death was naught, life was naught; Force only existed." The story of Vanamee is a testimony to the mysterious power of love and the renewal of life, the story of Presley a discovery of the power of economic force. In both cases some power is presumed to exist in ways that are beyond man's control and to operate, ultimately, for the good of mankind. A grand transcendental law of compensation seems to embrace life in both its spiritual and material aspects. Vanamee's religious mysticism and the naturalistic philosophy glimpsed by Presley are like two parts of a chorus commenting upon the tragedy of Magnus Derrick and the epic of the ranchers' struggle. Heroism and tragedy exist, they say, but they are really only a passing show and witness of the pitiful and fitful glory of being human. The abundant harvest that is gathered from the San Joaquin Valley, in spite of the conflict of men, suggests a force or a fate above man that gets the necessary work of the world done. To ancient peoples the grain was an expression of a divine reality, and so it appears to be to Norris; the penultimate paragraph of the *Octopus* reads:

> But the WHEAT remained. Untouched, unassailable, undefiled, that mighty world-force, that nourisher of nations, wrapped in Nirvanic calm, indifferent to the human swarm, gigantic, resistless, moved onward in its appointed grooves. Through the welter of blood at the irrigating ditch, through the sham charity and shallow philanthropy of famine-relief committees, the great harvest of Los Muertos rolled like a flood from the Sierras to the Himalayas to feed thousands of starving scarecrows on the barren plains of India.

The wheat is a great god holding out hope to man and signifying that life only avails.

The renewal of life is the grand theme of *The Octopus*. The land and the growing wheat its most moving images. Norris was not altogether happy in the symbol he chose for the menace of the railroad. The octopus may satisfactorily represent the abstract power of the railroad as a business trust reaching its greedy tentacles across the land and sucking down men and wealth into its "ever-hungry maw," but it is not a suitable image for use in narrative passages. The railroad engine, imagined as a one-eyed horse—a bellowing, charging, galloping monster—must be brought into service when dramatic action is involved. On two occasions at least, at the close of the first and last chapters, the metaphor is mixed, and we have both the galloping monster and the monster with tentacles. Norris's groping for the key images of his work suggests the kind of imagination that accumulates rather than refines materials, that pushes together disparate elements instead of separating them. The mixed horse-octopus image shows the same eclecticism as the use of parallel heroes and heroines, the mixture of four genres, and the combining of both spiritual and materialistic philosophies of life. In all these respects—imagery, characterization, form, and theme—Norris's imagination gathers and expands in a manner and on a scale like that of Melville in *Moby-Dick*. In *McTeague* we find an opposite tendency: Norris stays close to a dramatic symbolical center and develops it minutely and exhaustively through repetition. In *The Octopus* it is his ambition to fill the encyclopedic form of the epic. Great range, variety, and magnitude of action Norris succeeds in getting, but his attempt to adapt his prose style to accord with his epic subject must be accounted a failure. When his language was crude and raw, as it naturally tended to be, it creates in his people an appropriate quality, described by Howells as "something rankly, earthy, and elemental in them, which gives them the pathos of tormented Titans." [17] But the description of the land, the apostrophes to wheat, the hushed poetic tones in the romance of Vanamee are done in a style that "degenerates colossally into bombast." [18] Awkwardness

of language in *McTeague* has at least the virtue of
building the impression of a crude environment and set
of characters; in *The Octopus* it works against the sharp
definition of epic objectivity.

Style was perhaps beyond Norris's control; heroism
was a problem he wrestled with consciously. From one
point of view *The Octopus* is a study in the possibilities
of heroism and asks these questions: What are the varie-
ties of heroism? Of what avail is heroism in an age given
to commercial activity? The answer seems to be that
heroism avails nothing, that men merely serve issues
in an ineffectual way and might better take Emerson's
warning to heart: "Foolish hands may mix and mar; /
Wise and sure the issues are." Magnus Derrick's leadership ends in his ruin, Annixter's new life is abruptly cut
off because of his participation in the cause, and Presley reaches only a stage of prospective commitment.
Presley's failure to pursue the heroic course of Derrick
and Annixter reflects the skepticism that Norris seems
to feel about heroic action after the incident at the culvert when six men are killed in the shooting between
the ranchers and the sheriff's party. After fumbling
their way into violence, both sides are appalled by the
bloody outcome. Suddenly the fervent determination
of the ranchers to wage war against the railroad seems
inappropriate and their campaign begins to flag. The
zest with which Norris describes the conflict up to that
point is, for the remaining quarter of the book, replaced by a distinct distaste for violence and a growing
conviction that nothing can be done to stop the in-
exorable force of economic process. Inconsistently, Norris still continues to call attention to the injustice of
the railroad's practices. In chapter 8, book two, he
presents a series of scenes that alternate between a
starving family of railroad victims and a feasting family
of wealthy people, and in the very last chapter we are

treated to an account of the accidental freak death of
S. Behrman. Through the ironical juxtaposition of social conditions, a device that is the stock-in-trade of social protest writers, and through the melodramatic pun-
ishment of the "villain," Norris has his say about the
justice of the ranchers' cause and the evil of the railroad even though his naturalistic philosophy forbids
him to make a more direct statement. Justice is done in
part, but not through the agency of heroes. Still, the
characters commend themselves to us for their gravity
and dignity as they move in an atmosphere that sur-
rounds even their most petty activities with awe. In
The Octopus, as in *Moby-Dick*, we have the anomaly of
a work combining heroic narrative with an underlying
prejudice against heroism.

It is a paradox of epic literature that while its primary
end is to celebrate the heroic deeds of great men, its
underlying tone is a melancholy awareness of man's
inevitable failure. Even Virgil, who was as much excited about the grand designs of men as a poet could
be, recognized that there were "tears in things." Norris
is in this tradition, his naturalistic philosophy casting
the same shadow over the exploits of men as the fate
of earlier epic poets. His epic novel daringly presents the
great inchoate body of the world as Wheat, which is
regulated by two laws, economic and biologic: economic law determines the production and distribution
of wheat, biologic law assures the renewal of life on
earth and among men. These are the two principles between which man oscillates, as between two mighty
primeval gods, breaking himself in heroic defiance of
one and mending himself in worshipful reliance upon
the other.

3

The Grapes of Wrath

The line of descent from *The Octopus* to *The Grapes of Wrath* is as direct as any that can be found in American literature. The journey of the Okies in Steinbeck's book is certainly in the spirit of one of those "various fightings westward" that Norris identified as productive of epic writing: "Just that long and terrible journey from the Mississippi to the ocean is an epic in itself." [1] As one would expect, too, the later book reflects a more advanced stage of economic development, presenting as it does the struggle of proletarian masses against capitalist power, while the conflict in *The Octopus* is between two parties of the owning class, the ranchers, or small entrepreneurs, against the trust. Both novels have a universalizing tendency in that they create from a local situation a synecdoche of worldwide import. Thus Steinbeck's Okies, having all the surface characteristics of rural Americans of a certain region, are essentially farmers suddenly reduced by natural catastrophe and economic process to the status of unskilled laborers. Theirs is a cataclysmic predicament of the twentieth century. In the course of the journey imposed upon them they learn to identify themselves as a separate class and then to discover and develop leaders who will guide them in their effort to reestablish themselves in society. *The Grapes of Wrath* is a thoroughly didactic epic novel: an exploited group discovers that it is being exploited, that it is, indeed, a new class in society, the proletariat; individuals within that class discover the manner of that exploitation and grope for the means to combat it, or at least protest it; and the reader of the book, presumably, discovers that an alarming world economic condition is now making itself felt in America. The novel has a two-part theme, the education of a people and the education of its emerging leaders, and a three-part action, the dispossession, migration, and re-settlement of a people.

To dignify his starving sharecroppers and give form to their story, Steinbeck draws upon two epic traditions of migratory peoples, the account of the Israelites in the Book of Exodus and the story of the Trojans in the *Aeneid*. From the New Testament and the epic tradition he derives the forms of heroism and self-sacrifice that inspire the leaders of these people. Criticism has taken more note of the Bible influence because it is so obvious: there are unmistakable parallels between the trials of the Okies and the Israelites, between preacher Casy and Christ, and between Tom Joad and Moses. It is not surprising that Steinbeck's language is a close imitation of the English of the King James Version. A result of his deliberate effort to adapt style to subject in all his works, it constitutes a much more successful solution to the problem of creating a special style for an epic novel than Norris's romantic colors in *The Octopus*. To obtain elevation of style Steinbeck poeticizes his prose by echoing the phrasing and vocabulary of the King James Version in his descriptive passages and, secondly, by endowing the low-colloquial speeches of Casy and Tom Joad with an unusual amount of passion, imagery, and philosophical comment. As an example of the first method, here is the opening paragraph of chapter 17, one of the interchapters:

> The cars of the migrant people crawled out of the side roads onto the great cross-country highway, and

they took the migrant way to the West. In the daylight they scuttled like bugs to the westward; and as the dark caught them, they clustered like bugs near to shelter and to the water. And because they were lonely and perplexed, because they had all come from a place of sadness and worry and defeat, and because they were all going to a new mysterious place, they huddled together; they talked together; they shared their lives, their food, and the things they hoped for in the new country. Thus it might be that one family camped near a spring, and another camped for the spring and for company, and a third because two families had pioneered the place and found it good. And when the sun went down, perhaps twenty families and twenty cars were there.[2]

Employing Biblical devices more thickly than most, this passage indicates what Steinbeck is seeking to do and the means he uses. Dignity and solemnity are imparted to the miserable plight of the Okies by triadic phrasing, augmentations such as "near to" and "it might be," repetitions of word and phrase, and exact echoes such as "found it good." Association with the Bible story of the Israelites through language alone leads considerable elevation to the Okies. In his second method of aggrandizing the prose style of his novel, Steinbeck tries to intensify with poetic expressiveness the crude speech of his Okies. The result, as illustrated in an informal sermon by Casy, resembles the style of Huck Finn in his lyrical moments:

"I ain't sayin' I'm like Jesus," the preacher went on. "But I got tired like Him, an' I got mixed up like Him, an' I went into the wilderness like Him, without no campin' stuff. Nighttime I'd lay on my back an' look up at the stars; morning I'd set an' watch the sun come up; midday I'd look out from a hill at the rollin' country; evenin' I'd foller the sun down. Sometimes I'd pray like I always done. On'y I couldn' figure what I was prayin' to or for. There was the hills, an' there was me, an' we wasn't separate no more. We was one thing. An' that one thing was holy." (P. 110)

Between these two extremes, the thick Biblical and the poetic low colloquial, lies the narrative style in which the bulk of the Joads' story is told. It retains some of the deliberate rhythm of the Biblical and some of the realistic vocabulary of the colloquial styles. The three styles make a blend, one style modulating well with another. There is no weakness in the book on that score, but there is some question about the appropriateness of the exalted styles altogether. Just as in the ritual behavior of the Okies, so in the exalted language that describes them and in the impassioned speech that they sometimes use, there is considerable pompousness. In both gesture and speech Steinbeck occasionally comes too near to a burlesque tone; his seriousness becomes excessive, and he commits the prime error of many writers who attempt the epic, swelling and grandiose-ness. He lifts the Joads, in particular, and the Okies, in general, too quickly and abruptly from their realistic existence to the level of epic heroism.

There is no question of the influence of the Old and New Testaments on *The Grapes of Wrath*. Parallels with the *Aeneid* are hardly as deliberate, but are worth pointing out as evidence that the whole ancient heroic tradition contributes to the materials of the epic novel. In the American work the three-part narrative scheme of the *Aeneid* appears again in the record of a people who lose their homeland, make a perilous journey to a promising new land, and fight against the hostile natives there for a chance to begin a new life. The first two parts are more tightly woven than the third because the family stays very close together as they leave home and travel the road across the country, but after their arrival in California the pressures pulling them apart multiply. Uncle John's guilt gets worse, Rosasharn's time is drawing near, Al's desire to strike out for himself is intensified, the youngsters Ruthie and Winfield are less controllable, Casy and Tom are being drawn into the larger community. The Joad family's mode of travel, the improvised car-truck piled high with household goods, can no longer serve as a striking central image after the journey is over and the family lives in a more complicated social setting. The result of all this individual stress and social complication is an increased variety of material and a more episodic structure in the third part of the novel. There is still a strong line of action in the economic struggle, but it does not have the clear goal of the earlier drive towards freedom in the West. The same blurring of the narrative line, the same sense of confused action, is to be noted in the last part of the *Aeneid*; but whereas this falling-off of intensity is a fault in the *Aeneid* because it does not accord with the triumph of Trojan arms, in the novel it is in perfect accord with the frustration of Okie ambitions. Undoubtedly, interest in the third part of the *Aeneid* flags because attention is turned away from sharply focused individuals, Aeneas himself and Dido, to more generalized accounts of tribes and warring nations. Similarly, in *The Grapes of Wrath* the exclusive interest in the family sustains the first two parts better than the last part, in which there is a scattering of interest among larger social units.

Narrative structure is the most accomplished aspect of *The Grapes of Wrath*. Steinbeck achieves a successful solution to the chief structural problem of the epic writer, whether it be Homer or Tolstoy: the harmonization of the general social action involving masses of people and major issues with particular actions involving closely examined individuals and their concerns. Steinbeck simplifies his problem somewhat by restricting himself to the members of one family and their few close associates, Casy and the Wilsons, and to a few quickly drawn agents of their enemies. His Joads serve the same synecdochic purpose of Zola's Maheus in *Germinal,* but it is to be noted that Zola does not confine himself to one side of the struggle alone nor to one family of miners. The Joads exemplify in detail what is presumably going on in thousands of similar families. Moreover, Steinbeck supplies a more explicit link between the general and particular actions by using "interchapters" or panoramic narrative in which the activities of all the Okies are summarized, sometimes from an objective viewpoint and sometimes as collective monologue from the viewpoint of representative Okies. Enough details are common to both kinds of action to give the sense that the Joads are living the same kind of life and having the same thoughts and feelings as the masses described in the interchapters. Except for the interruption they make in the story of the Joads, the interchapters are readily assimilated for their thematic and material relevance.

A few minor echoes from classical epics may be cited. The patriarch of the family whose fortunes we follow, the Joads, has to be carried onto the truck when they are forced to leave home; he dies on the way, and a pause in the journey is made to bury him with solemn rites in a strange land. After the feast of pork and potatoes, Ma Joad declares, "Grampa—it's like he's dead a year." A granddaughter consoles the dead man's grieving old wife; she lies "beside the old woman and the murmur of their soft voices drifted to the fire" where the men were sitting. At the place where Grampa dies the Joads make friends with another family of Okies, the Wilsons, whose car has broken down. The two Joad boys undertake to repair it and they find the necessary parts in an auto graveyard presided over by a one-eyed "specter of a man," who cries miserably as he tells them his sad plight. This scene, according to an early commentator on Steinbeck, "afterwards floats in the mind like a piece of epic." [3] The car is repaired and the two families now join forces as they proceed on their journey together. These are but faint echoes of the story of Aeneas's father, Aeneas at Eryx, and Odysseus's tale of Polyphemus.

The ceremonial solemnity with which the Joads perform certain family functions suggests a more general epic quality. The frequent family councils, the ritual killing of the pigs before the departure, the burial of Grampa, and many other activities are executed by Steinbeck's American sharecroppers with all of the ponderous care and sacred protocol of noblemen out of the heroic tradition of the past. Such attempts to aggrandize the folk, also to be found in *The Octopus* and *For Whom the Bell Tolls*, often fall into bathos in Steinbeck. Much more effectively done are the many prophecies of disaster uttered all along the road to California, particularly one by a kind of Teiresias whom the Joads meet in one of the improvised campsites. A "ragged man," his coat a mass of "torn streamers," he at first refuses to say what lies in store for the Joads in California. "I don' wanna fret you," he tells Pa. What he finally does reveal is exactly what happens to the Joads in the remaining half of the book—their being exploited in an economic situation in which thousands of men compete for a few jobs. He finishes his prophecy, "and then he turned and walked quickly away into the darkness."

Jim Casy is a prophet in another, more hopeful,

tradition, that of Christ in the New Testament. Disturbed by the economic plight of the farming class he serves as a Baptist preacher, he makes a retreat in order to ponder their situation and decides that he cannot help by continuing in the ministry. Actually, his Christianity is simply broadened by the sudden growth of his social consciousness. He becomes inspired with the idea that the brotherhood of all men must work together for social justice, and to this he adds a more abstract idea of the holy relatedness of mankind in a kind of Emersonian oversoul.[4] This doctrine he preaches as a new revelation to save the Okies from destruction and the world from economic warfare. He dies preaching for the cause and saying to his assailants, "You don' know what you're a-doin!" But he leaves behind a disciple in Tom Joad, who at once begins to tell the story of Casy and even thinks he sees him after his death.

If Casy is Christian and socialist, Ma Joad is pagan and primitive. If Casy adds the spirit of a New Testament prophet to the doctrine of a twentieth-century class-conscious revolutionary, Ma Joad is in the ancient tradition of the kore-goddess protecting her hero-son and her people. She is splendidly revealed (*dea certe*) to Tom when he returns home, a stranger, after spending four years in prison for having killed a man in a quarrel:

> Her full face was not soft; it was controlled, kindly. Her hazel eyes seemed to have experienced all possible tragedy and to have mounted pain and suffering like steps into a high calm and a superhuman understanding. She seemed to know, to accept, to welcome her position, the citadel of the family, the strong place that could not be taken. . . . And from her great and humble position in the family she had taken dignity and a clean calm beauty. From her position as healer, her hands had grown sure and cool

and quiet; from her position as arbiter she had become as remote and faultless in judgment as a goddess.

She moved toward him lithely, soundlessly in her bare feet, and her face was full of wonder. Her small hand felt his arm, felt the soundness of his muscles. And then her fingers went up to his cheek as a blind man's fingers might. And her joy was nearly like sorrow. . . . (Pp. 100–101)

The only embrace between mother and wandering son is the touch of her hand to his face; between mother-goddess and human son is the same gulf that we see between Venus and Aeneas in book one of the *Aeneid*: "Oh, why may we not join/Hand to hand, or ever converse straightforwardly?" Like Pilar in *For Whom the Bell Tolls*, like Dilsey in *The Sound and the Fury*, Ma Joad is richly endowed with the awesome, divine presence of the goddess who presides over the generations of the family and the cycle of life. Her every action—except one, as we shall see—is motivated by the instinctive desire to keep the family together for the purpose of mere survival. She cradles the dying Granma Joad in her arms, she protects and nourishes her pregnant daughter, she restores her son Tom to life.

Produced by the influences of a Christ-like companion, Casy, and his mother-goddess, Tom Joad is indeed a hero of divine origin. He is moved to heroic acts by the spirit of anger and revenge which the murder of Casy stirs in him, and on the other hand by the spirit of compassion and love for mankind which his mother so well demonstrates in her selfless devotion to the family. Images of death and rebirth mark Tom's relations with Casy and Ma Joad, as in their different ways they strive to bring him to the role of a hero. There is something terribly grim and sad about the career of Tom. Never allowed a romantic interlude, he is plunged into the troubles of his people upon his return from prison and slowly comes to an awareness of his responsibilities of leadership. Almost glumly, with little expression of personal feeling, he does not only what is expected of him but more besides. A peak in his development occurs when, in the manner of a classic brother-in-arms, Tom at once kills the strikebreaker who has killed Casy; Tom is then himself struck, escapes from his pursuers, and comes to an irrigation ditch, where he bathes his torn cheek and nose. Casy, when he was a preacher, used to baptize people in irrigation ditches; he is killed as he stands beside a stream. Tom's introduction to the bitter struggle of worker against producer dates from the violent experience beside the stream. The stinging baptism at the irrigation ditch, after he has fled, does not lead him into his new life at once, however. He must die before he can be wholly reborn, and he must make a retreat to consecrate himself to the cause in his soul as well as in his arm and receive the blessing of his goddess-mother as well as the example of his surrogate father. He rejoins the family, but because he is being sought by the police and can easily be identified by his wounds, he must remain hidden: he is as one who no longer exists in the Joad family. To get past the guards who are looking for him, he lies between two mattresses in the Joad truck, and then he takes refuge in the brush near the boxcar that the family is now inhabiting. After Ruthie has told her playmates about her big brother Tom, Ma decides that she must release Tom from his obligation to the family for his own safety, and she goes to the "cave of vines" he has improvised. Tom, in the meantime, has come around to a sense of his duty to "fight so hungry people can eat" and is ready to begin a new life away from the family.

The scene in which Ma and Tom part is the climax of Tom's career as a hero and the very heart of Steinbeck's point that class must replace family as the social unit worth fighting for. It is a high point in Steinbeck's writing, and some of its strength comes from the association of rebirth imagery and myths of the mother-goddess and her hero son with the crude story of an organizer of farm labor in twentieth-century America. Carrying a dish of "pork chops and fry potatoes," Ma walks at night "to the end of the line of tents" in the camp of fruit pickers and steps "in among the willows beside the stream" until she reaches "the black round hole of the culvert where she always left Tom's food." She leaves her package at the hole and waits a little distance away, among the willows:

> And then a wind stirred the willows delicately, as though it tested them, and a shower of golden leaves coasted down to the ground. Suddenly a gust boiled in and racked the trees, and a cricking downpour of leaves fell. Ma could feel them on her hair and on her shoulders. Over the sky a plump black cloud moved, erasing the stars. The fat drops of rain scattered down, splashing loudly on the fallen leaves, and the cloud moved on and unveiled the stars again. Ma shivered. The wind blew past and left the thicket quiet, but the rushing of the trees went on down the stream. (P. 567)

A "dark figure" finally appears at the culvert; it is Tom and after her plea to talk with him he leads Ma to his hideout, across a stream and a field filled with "the blackening stems" of cotton plants. Ma crawls into the "cave of vines" and there in the dark they talk. She explains that she did not let him go earlier because she was afraid for him; with the touch of her hand she discovers that he has a bad scar on his face and his nose is crooked. Again, as in the first scene of recognition between mother and son, the hand of the mother lingers lovingly on the face of the son, just as Thetis "took her son's head in her arms" before she releases him for battle in book 18 of the *Iliad*. Ma Joad forces her gift of seven dollars on Tom to help him on his perilous way. Full of his new mission in life, he does not respond to the love his mother expresses for him, but simply says, "Goodby." Ma returns to the camp, and Tom presumably will go on to his doom as Casy did before him but also to a sort of immortality for men who have fought for social justice:

> "Then I'll be all aroun' in the dark. I'll be ever'where —wherever you look. Wherever they's a fight so hungry people can eat, I'll be there. Wherever they's a cop beatin' up a guy, I'll be there. If Casy knowed, why, I'll be in the way guys yell when they're mad an'—I'll be in the way kids laugh when they're hungry an' they know supper's ready. An' when our folks eat the stuff they raise an' live in the houses they build—why, I'll be there." (P. 572)

This is a kind of immortality that Ma "don' un'erstan'," although it is she who confers it on him by making his heroism possible.

It is not enough to say that this wonderful scene is inspired by the New Testament story of Christ's resurrection from the tomb.[5] The "cave of vines" and the tomb are the womb from which the hero is delivered to a new life, but the landscape in Steinbeck's scene is more nearly that of the classical underworld. The nourishing of the hero-son by the earth-goddess mother until he is strong enough to leave her suggests the myth of Ishtar and Tammuz, and the commitment of the son to war and eventual death recalls the sad exchange between Thetis and Achilles. Tom Joad's "death" brings an end to his ordinary existence as one of thousands of Okies; he is reborn into the life of the epic hero, who dooms himself to an early death as soon as he elects a heroic course of action. His consecration is affirmed by his discipleship to Casy and the ritual release performed by his mother. If there is a resurrection, it is the resurrection of Casy in Tom. Tom's rebirth through the agency of Casy and Ma Joad has a striking antecedent in the experience of Henry Fleming in Crane's *Red Badge of Courage*. The change in Henry's attitude toward heroism—from callow sentimentality to a mature sense of its real consequences—is in part wrought by the example of Jim Conklin, another Christ-like figure, and Henry's encounter with death in the forest, alone, and rebirth among his comrades.[6]

The rebirth of Tom as hero is emphasized by the ironical implication of another incident. Shortly after Ma Joad has returned from the stream and the willows, the pregnant Rosasharn distractedly seeks refuge in the very same place, along "the stream and the trail that went beside it." She lies down among the berry vines and feels "the weight of the baby inside her." Not long after this the rains come. Pa Joad and other men in the camp work feverishly to hold back the swollen stream from flooding their miserable living quarters; they build an earth embankment, but it is swept away and the water washes into the camp. At the same time Ma Joad and some neighboring women are helping Rosasharn deliver her baby, but they meet with no greater success—the baby is stillborn. Uncle John is delegated to bury the "blue shriveled little mummy"; instead, he takes the apple box it is in and floats it down the river, hoping that it will be a sign to the California landowners of the Okies' sore affliction. "Go down an' tell 'em," he says, in words echoing the Negro spiritual "Go Down, Moses" and thus linking three oppressed peoples—Israelites, American Negro slaves, and the Okies. The river is the same that saw the rebirth of Tom, who is a kind of Moses to his people, and now it receives the dead infant.

In Tom the Biblical and epic traditions of the hero

came together to make a proletarian leader of the
twentieth century. The man of anger and the quick blow
of revenge is also the disciple devoted to self-sacrifice in
the cause of the downtrodden and deprived. The son of
the spouse-goddess is released from the death that is the
family in order to do battle for the class that will possess
the future. The man of violence bred from personal
pride—Tom killed his first man in a tavern brawl—is
baptized in the violence of class struggle, and he turns,
like the classical hero, from the defense of his own
rights to the defense of all men's rights. Like Presley
in *The Octopus*, Tom is an apprentice-hero who learns
from a man more experienced in warfare, in class
warfare. What Presley learns from his mentor, the
anarchist barkeep, is in the same political tradition as
what Tom learns from Casy; the leftist attack on
capitalism is rejected by Norris, however, and seemingly
accepted by Steinbeck after it is filtered through
Christian feeling and presented in Biblican and epic
images.

The Grapes of Wrath begins with a drought bringing
death to the land and dispossession to its inhabitants
and ends ironically with a flood that again destroys the
land and disperses the people. Nature as well as society
dooms the Okies, who fall from one catastrophe into
another, losing their land, their belongings, their livelihood, and finally even their miserable shelters. But in
spite of homelessness and despair, the Joads have succeeded in making an important journey, passing from
one bond, the family, to another, mankind. "They's
changes—all over," it is said. "Use' ta be the fambly was
fust. It ain't so now. It's anybody." In place of the
family a new form of social organization is tentatively
envisaged on the model of a small socialist community.
Not all can see the promised land—only Casy, who does
not live to enter it, and Tom, who is on the verge of

entering it at the close of the book. Pa Joad's symbolical attempt, in fighting the river, to unite the community after the old style of neighborly cooperation comes too late and fails. Having long since relinquished control of the family to Ma, Pa Joad is a man without a role to play in the world. He joins Magnus Derrick in the company of those in the older generation who, unable to accommodate themselves to a new situation, are only pitifully heroic. Others, those who seek individual solutions, are shown to be equally futile. Muley Graves stays on the abandoned farmlands in Oklahoma and must live "like a coyote" on the trash left behind and the wild animals still surviving on the plains. Uncle Noah wanders away down a river he half-wittedly fancies, and Uncle John gets drunk when he can sneak the money. Al, Tom's younger brother, strikes out for himself, ironically to start another hapless family. While Ma cannot understand Tom's social idealism, she and Rosasharn do come around to the side of humanity in the closing scene of the book when Rosasharn, with her mother's prompting, feeds to a dying old man, a stranger, the milk her body had stored for her child. With neither child nor husband Rosasharn must abandon the idea of family. Ma's family has disintegrated, Rosasharn's has not even had a chance to begin.

The images of the community and the hero that dominate the ending of *The Grapes of Wrath* are pitiful enough: a fugitive coming out of hiding to do unequal battle with an infinitely superior enemy and two frightened women trying desperately to save a dying old man in an empty barn. It seems to be an image of miserable survival in the face of awesome odds. Still, out of the sordid circumstances of a purely naturalistic life a hero is born in a manner reminiscent of great heroes of the past. The affirmation of a better future seems groundless, but there is affirmation nonetheless, and a hero is ready to attempt its achievement by leading people who have prepared themselves for a new kind of society. "The book is neither riddle nor tragedy," insists Warren French, "it is an epic comedy of the triumph of the 'holy spirit.' " [7]

Norris explores the possibilities of heroism in one novel, Steinbeck and Hemingway in a whole succession of novels. Steinbeck seems to want to believe in heroic behavior and the ideal community, yet in one novel after another he submits a negative report as to the chances of either in our time. His first novel, *Cup of Gold* (1929), in Warren French's summary, "asserts that there is no place for the swashbuckling hero in the modern world." [8] In *Tortilla Flat* (1935) Steinbeck lovingly presents the irregular habits and amusing antics of a number of paisanos, but at the same time, by stressing a mock-heroic parallel with Malory's *Morte d'Arthur*, he insists upon our viewing their attempts to be heroic as ridiculous. In the end, Danny, the Arthur of a paisano Round Table, armed with a broken table leg, goes out to do battle and dies in a duel with "The Enemy" in the "gulch," a place which he and his companions used for want of an outhouse. Although the hero in the next novel, *In Dubious Battle* (1936), bears a slight resemblance to another figure from the Arthurian legend, Percival, the mood of this work is starkly naturalistic. Jim Nolan's attempt to become the leader of embattled laborers is soon ended by the blast of a shotgun that renders him, horribly and quite literally, a hero without a face. His epitaph is spoken by his mentor, Mac, and is necessarily brief: "Comrades! He didn't want nothing for himself—." Lennie, the hero in *Of Mice and Men* (1937), is a feebleminded giant, "shapeless of face," and obviously incapable of responsible behavior. In his time of trouble he takes refuge in a place near a river where a path winds "through the willows and among the sycamores." But Lennie is not reborn there; his best friend must become his executioner there because Lennie cannot control the great strength he has and is consequently a menace to the community.

In *The Grapes of Wrath*, for the first time, Steinbeck offers a not altogether forlorn image of the epic hero. Tom Joad is a hero with a face, badly battered though it is; he survives the assault upon him, his spirit is revived at a place where willows grow by a stream and, presumably, he is embarked upon a heroic career. Jim Nolan finishes before he ever really begins, and the possibility of rebirth never materializes. Just before his death Mac advises him of a place of refuge should the occasion ever arise, "a deep cave" hidden by willows near a stream. But Jim never gets to the cave; he dies actually, not symbolically as Tom does. Nor does Jim have Ma Joad as his protective goddess and Casy as his martyred mentor. Mac, a hardheaded and cautious labor organizer, does not have the mythical credentials to inspire a hero. Lennie also has a cave to retire to if he becomes too much of a burden to his friend George, but there is no returning from it. Only Tom returns from the cave and the willows, the place of death, to present the face of a hero to the world, a face so badly scarred that he can no longer be recognized as Tom Joad. Of all Steinbeck's heroes, he is the only one who affirms the possibility of a hero arising out of the anonymity of twentieth-century economic strife and still bearing the signs of an ancient dedication.

4

For Whom the Bell Tolls

It is not surprising that both *The Grapes of Wrath* and *For Whom the Bell Tolls* express a militant sense of social responsibility: they were published within a year of each other at the close of a decade in American life that saw a remarkable extension of social action on the part of the government and the beginning of a new war era requiring of Americans the utmost sacrifice for the common cause. One novel is a lesson in social responsibility in economic strife, the other a lesson in responsibility in warfare. Through these works Steinbeck and Hemingway were quite consciously responding to the needs of the time. As it turned out, Hemingway's book has remained more topical since it had the good fortune of appearing just at the time when American energies were turning from social to military efforts, which have not yet ceased; while Steinbeck's book applied itself to economic problems which have not become as serious as the problem of war. But though the subjects and impacts are different, the didactic burden is the same: both books advance the thesis that a wider and stronger social commitment is imperative in the contemporary world. The Okies learn that primitive family loyalty is not sufficient to cope with modern economic problems; the Spanish partisans learn that they must fight not only for the survival of their own little band but for the national cause, indeed for the cause of freedom and decency throughout the world. The Joads have great difficulty learning this lesson, and some members of the family never do. The guerillas—including one from the most independent groups of people, a gypsy—learn almost too easily, laying down their lives with the utmost courage and dedication. Lionel Trilling calls them creatures of a writer with "a romantic sense of the social and personal virtues" and finds them comparable to Cooper's Indians.[1] The Scottish retainers in Scott's border novels also come to mind. All have the loyalty and stolid simplicity of lesser figures in epic writing of the modern era.

One essential difference in the fictional worlds created by Steinbeck and Hemingway is that Steinbeck is always deeply concerned with the community as well as with the hero while Hemingway is primarily concerned with the hero. It is most fitting that *The Grapes of Wrath* closes with a picture of the remnants of a community—a dying man, a hysterical boy, a childless woman, and a mother—and *For Whom the Bell Tolls* with the hero alone, abandoned by his companions. Equally important with his search for a proletarian hero is Steinbeck's lifelong search for a viable community of men. Often he can find nothing better than the mock-heroic society of paisanos in *Tortilla Flat*, the bums and prostitutes of *Sweet Thursday*, the four outcasts in *Of Mice and Men* who dream of living together on an ideal farm that will never be. Finally, in *In Dubious Battle* and *The Grapes of Wrath* a community worthy of serious consideration is found, agricultural workers and farmers who are readying themselves to do battle for their economic existence. Great care is expended in both books to trace the incipient development of a new kind of community, a proletariat.

The failure of community life in the modern world led Hemingway to create small select groups living within a hostile society—the expatriates in *The Sun Also Rises*, for example—but these function as settings for his heroes rather than as experiments of community life or centers of revolutionary dissent. Hemingway's one ideal community, the band of guerillas in *For Whom the Bell Tolls*, is only a cell within a larger grouping, the Loyalist Army, which is shown to be full of imperfections and corruption. These groups are of much less interest to Hemingway than their leaders, who are studied on every level, from General Golz at the top of the military hierarchy to El Sordo, the leader of four men. The complexities Hemingway discovers in them arise from balancing their heroic potentialities in the scale with the circumstances of contemporary warfare. The case of Robert Jordan, the only American on the scene, receives the most attention. To what extent, Hemingway seems to be asking, can a man with twentieth-century sensibilities behave like an epic hero of the past? How will his political skepticism sort with devotion to a cause, his habit of withdrawal with the need for cooperation, his psychological disabilities with the necessity to act decisively? What balance can be struck between personal honor and social responsibility, between his modern emphasis on sexual gratification and the act of self-sacrifice? The answers to these questions are to be found in the characterization of Jordan, and the answers do not resolve the paradoxes, for we find that Jordan can be both skeptical and unquestioning, moved both by personal and social honor, accept love and reject it. Jordan is a more deeply troubled hero than any of his precursors but not so troubled that he cannot reconcile the past with the present.

Selfless devotion to a cause and self-sacrifice are conceived in both Steinbeck and Hemingway as substitutes for religion. Doc Burton, the skeptical observer of *In Dubious Battle*, likes to remind the champions of social justice that they are moved by religious feeling, and Lady Brett in *The Sun Also Rises* believes that "deciding not to be a bitch," by which she means giving up her lover for his own good, is "sort of what we have instead of God." Jim Casy, who first takes fire with the idea of social responsibility in *The Grapes of Wrath*, keeps insisting that he is no longer a Christian preacher, yet his religious spirit continues to impress people no matter what the content of his preaching and he is undoubtedly a Christ figure in his death. Casy has simply transferred the ideal of Christian charity and self-sacrifice from the church and parish to the marketplace. Similarly, Pilar links religion and the social sense when she says, "Every one needs to talk to some one. . . . Before we had religion and other nonsense. Now for every one there should be some one to whom one can speak frankly, for all the valor that one could have one becomes very alone." To which Jordan replies, "We are not alone. We are all together." But this is a thought that Jordan finds it necessary to repeat often, for he is not altogether convinced that valor is not entirely sufficient. He must keep reminding himself that it is the cause as well as his honor for which he is risking his life. The talk he hears at Gaylord's, the hotel in Madrid frequented by correspondents and high Russian officials, puts a strain on his faith in the revolutionary movement. But he allays his doubts by recollecting that at the headquarters of the International Brigade one had "a feeling of consecration to a duty toward all of the oppressed of the world which would be as difficult and embarrassing to speak about as religious experience and yet it was authentic." At the headquarters of the International Brigade and the Fifth Regiment, "you felt that you were taking part in a crusade. That was the only word for it although it was a word that had been so worn and abused that it no longer gave its true meaning." Ten years after Lieutenant Henry had scorn-fully dismissed such words as "sacred, glorious, and sacrifice," Robert Jordan, the Hemingway hero in epic dress, revives a word that subsumes them all, crusade. In spite of some doubts about absolute justice being on the side of the Loyalists and their allies, Jordan has settled the matter in his mind definitely enough to allow him to act. The implication throughout his cogi-tations is that while the causes for which the twentieth-century hero is asked to die do not bear much thinking about, the hero still must die for them. Unlike Lieuten-ant Henry, Jordan does not withdraw when he encount-ers the follies committed by men at war; his duty fixed, he does not indulge so much in the ironical view of life.

Much more serious are the doubts that the hero has about himself. These are reflected in the characteri-zations of Kashkin and Pablo. Kashkin was a dynamiter who had preceded Jordan in the mountains. Wounded in action against the Fascists and afraid of being captured and tortured, he had to ask Jordan to finish him off. Up to the very end of his dynamiting exploit Jordan lives in fear that he too will not be able to stand up to capture and torture, that out of cowardice he may commit suicide as his father did. Pablo is the guerilla whose leadership has been weakened by self-interest and the fear of death; he "puts his fox-hole before the interest of humanity." He is the fallen, inadequate hero whom Jordan, the apprentice-hero, might become if he allows his fear of death to take hold, if he is not *careful*, using the term in the Hemingway sense of keeping control over oneself in order not to go to pieces in times of great stress. After expressing his doubts about the advisability of blowing the bridge, after sulking, after stealing the detonator which is to be used in the task, Pablo finally does come around to the common cause. "I found myself too lonely," he explains, underlining the main theme of the book. He performs his part in the bridge-blowing with skill and courage, but as soon as the job is over he reverts to primitive peasant ways by killing his erstwhile comrades-in-arms, who are not from his band or native town, in order to get horses for men who are. It is not long after this that Jordan demonstrates the true role of the epic hero by giving up his life for strangers in a foreign land. Kashkin, the companion who has died before, and Pablo, the betrayer, are the two customary foils setting off the hero.

Jordan's education in heroism is well in advance of Presley's and Tom's. He is at the end of the hero's career which they are just starting. The political and economic conditions that strike Presley and Tom with shocking force have had their effect on Jordan long before the story begins, and when we meet him he is no longer actively concerned with these matters but devotes his most precise thinking to the special kind of prowess he must employ in battle, the strategy that will accomplish his mission, and the best deployment of the men at his disposal. Robert Jordan is Presley at the end of a longer development. Both young men want to write: Presley an epic about the West, Jordan a "true book" about Spain; both are impressed by leftist political doctrine: Presley from the anarchist Caraher, Jordan from Communists—and subsequently react against it; Presley botches his one attempt to use dynamite, Jordan is an expert dynamiter. In his readiness for action, in his prowess as a warrior, and in his devotion to duty, Jordan bears more resemblance to the traditional epic hero than any American hero in twentieth-century fiction. His modernness lies in his sensualism and in the fear he has of conducting himself in a cowardly way, of not being able to die well. The decision to die and the dying itself are of little consequence compared to the manner of his dying, which must be carried out with ritual precision. The whole book is an elaborate preparation for a death in the grand heroic style. In his lecture on Lincoln, Whitman was fond of saying that "the grand deaths of the race—the dramatic deaths of every nationality—are its most important inheritance-value." [2] In an era of mechanized and anonymous warfare, Hemingway sought to supply his countrymen with a hero who dies a glorious death, alone and facing not a host, nor machines as El Sordo must, but a troop of cavalry in a pine forest.

Carlos Baker argues that "Jordan is not to be scorned as the type of Achilles." [3] Indeed, his inner struggle is the same as Achilles': he must live with the knowledge that his death is fated to follow immediately upon the completion of his mission, and he must make a supreme effort to control himself, only with Jordan it is his fear that he must control and not his anger, which he calls "another damned luxury you can't afford." Achilles needs no help in facing death; it is in council that he is most deficient, and he must contain his anger in order to learn a civilized virtue, compassion. Jordan, however, can control his anger, and does so quite remarkably in the councils with the fractious Pablo and he does not lack compassion, as his friendship with the old man Anselmo proves, but he needs to rediscover the primitive hero's unflinching strength in the face of death. Like Achilles and other epic heroes Jordan resolves his personal problem in the course of a greater public action.

In Jordan there are echoes of other epic heroes besides Achilles. Certain externals of scene and action relate him quite closely to Roland. He has been assigned, by an admired commander, General Golz, to a kind of holding action in a mountain pass in Spain, a task that is very dangerous but which he undertakes without complaint and with insufficient numbers of soldiers. "We are too short of people but there is no sense to worry about that. I will do the bridge with what we have." When he learns that the enemy is prepared to meet the general attack, which will therefore fail, he dispatches a messenger to General Golz, "trying to put it so the attack would be cancelled, absolutely, yet convince them he wasn't trying to have it called off because of any fears he might have about the danger of his own mission." Honor moves Jordan just as surely and as absolutely as it does Roland. In the order of his loyalties it stands before the crusade against fascism and his love for Maria. Like Odysseus, Jordan is an outsider who employs others to help him in his dangerous task; he is crafty in his dealings with the guerillas and is careful to test each man's loyalty and capability. His task is long in preparing and quick in execution, thanks to his careful strategy and expert dispatch at the culminating moment. Like Aeneas, he enjoys an interlude of the love of a woman, whom he dismisses as soon as duty requires.

There is more emphasis on romantic love in *For Whom the Bell Tolls* than in any other American epic novel. Tom Joad is allowed absolutely no romantic interest, and Presley comes to an incipient feeling of love for Hilma only at the very end of the novel. Although it is oversentimental in its idyllic tone, the three-day romance of Jordan and Maria has traditional heroic patterns written into it. Profound mysteries are attached to the lovers' mating: "time absolutely still and they were both there, time having stopped and he felt the earth move out and away from under them." Maria's body is "magic" to Jordan, and he is amazed to find that in his association with this particular girl love and death are mingled. "When I am with Maria," he reflects, "I love her so that I feel, literally, as though I would die and I never believed in that nor thought that it could happen." The scene in which Jordan leaves Maria for battle is done in a manner reminiscent of the farewells of other epic heroes. In the chapter in *Moby-Dick* entitled "The Symphony," Ahab, certainly no great lover, still pauses to bid tender farewell to love and life on the eve of the fatal battle with the whale. On a "clear steel-blue day," when "air and sea were hardly separable in that all-pervading azure," Ahab lifts "his splintered helmet of a brow to the fair girl's forehead of heaven." Reversing conventional symbolism, Melville makes the sky feminine: "That glad, happy air, that winsome sky, did at last stroke and caress him; the step-mother world, so long cruel—forbidding—now threw affectionate arms round his stubborn neck, and did seem to joyously sob over him, as if over one, that however wilful and erring, she could yet find it in her heart to save and to bless." Sentimental imagery here does the work of narrative and tells the familiar story of the woman bidding farewell to the warrior who goes to his doom after a brief romance—as Ahab expresses it, "leaving but one dent in my marriage pillow." Never has Melville shown Ahab in such a soft mood as this, but then never is Homer more sentimental than in describing Hector taking leave of wife and child before battle. Far out at sea Ahab can only visualize his child awaking from a nap and his wife telling the boy "how I am abroad upon the deep, but will yet come back to dance him again." Then, like Hector, he discusses the role of fate in the lives of men: "Fate is the handspike."

Jordan, too, takes a warrior's leave of Maria soon after the first shot is fired on the day before his final battle. It is a day like Ahab's, "a lovely late spring morning." Maria is angry with Jordan when he firmly refuses to allow her to accompany him and orders her to return to the cave with Pilar. Then she relents, putting "both arms tight around his neck and kissed him." Later there is the famous scene in which the lovers part for good. To comfort Maria, Jordan invokes John Donne's notion of the identity of lovers' souls: "Thou wilt go now, rabbit. But I go with thee. As long as there is one of us there is both of us." We recall Tom Joad's idea that the fighter for social justice will live on wherever there is a fight to free men from oppression. Hemingway backs away from this to the romantic image of the immortality of lovers. But Jordan is really half-skeptical: "Try to believe what you told her," he tells himself, and a few moments later, as his death draws near, Maria is forgotten and Jordan is thinking, "I have fought for what I believe in for a year now. If we win here we win everywhere. The world is a fine place and worth the fighting for and I hate very much to leave it." Thus, in the best heroic tradition, Hemingway subordinates the romantic motive to the hero's sacrifice for duty and honor.

Far from being trivial, as some readers claim, the romantic interest in *For Whom the Bell Tolls* serves a very important thematic purpose. Maria is much more than a lover and survivor: she becomes a symbol of the cause for which Jordan and the partisans are fighting, or the essence of the cause that remains unambiguous and incontrovertible, the preservation of purity and innocence. While the political aspects of the Loyalist cause may come under suspicion, devotion to purity and innocence stands as the only absolutely fixed value. Paradoxically, war intensifies this devotion, Hemingway seems to be saying, and when all the killing and degradation is over only the devotion to innocence is worthy of mankind. The whole action at the bridge is an effort to make life possible for Maria and a heroic death possible for Jordan. Maria is the purpose of the communal effort, and everyone cooperates in doing what is best for her.

Maria is served by Pilar and Jordan in mysterious ways. Pilar is her protective goddess. It is she who insists

upon rescuing Maria from the Fascist train when everyone else regarded the girl as "something so sad and ugly
and apparenty worthless." She forces Pablo to cover the
retreat from the train, just as later Jordan covers the
retreat from the bridge to insure the escape of Maria.
Her acceptance of Jordan into the band is probably motivated unconsciously by her knowledge that Jordan will
replace Pablo as the hero caring for her precious charge.
Pilar's love for Maria is both that of a mother and a
lover; she is jealous of Jordan but knows that he is the
hero who will redeem Maria. Just before she surrenders
Maria to him she embraces her in a way that reminds us
of Ma Joad's farewell to Tom: "She stroked the girl's
head without looking down at her and ran a blunt
finger across the girl's forehead and then around the
line of her ear and down the line where the hair grew
on her neck" (p. 154). Pilar rescues Maria from death
and releases her to the life that Jordan has the power to
grant as her lover. His affair with Maria is a sort of
purification rite in which the true love of a hero removes
the burden of shame and the abomination of rape from
his beloved. In their first lovemaking Maria says, "And if
we do everything together, the other maybe never will
have been." (The Loathly Lady motif occurs again in
Brett's notion of the influence of Romero's love on her:
"He's wiped out that damned Cohn.") In a supra-
personal sense, Jordan, in offering his life for Maria's
sake, expiates for all mankind the sin of war, the great
destroyer of innocence.

Does Maria represent anything more than survival of
the innocent? Is she, like Angéle, whom she resembles
in several ways, a fertility figure as well? Some support
for this idea may be found in the imagery used to describe her hair. Occurring again and again, almost like
a leitmotif, is the description of her hair as "sun-
burned," "the color of ripe wheat," "the golden brown

of a grain field." But her hair is also closely cropped, like the hair of the sterile Brett. This, of course, is a result of the war and a temporary condition, but we learn that Maria wants to keep her hair as short as her lover's. Sometimes Maria's hair appears as a symbol of life that is brought into sharp contrast to the death-laden Jordan.[4] In his dying moments El Sordo reflects that "living was as a field of grain blowing in the wind"; Jordan loves to pass his hand through Maria's hair, and on the occasion when he first met her "he looked at her hair, that was thick and short and rippling when she passed her hand over it . . . as a grain field in the wind on a hillside." Jordan has Romero's sentimental belief that women should have long hair, yet Jordan does not "wish to bring either a son or a daughter into this world as this world is." Maria has the figure of a boy, she is compared to a colt; there is a suggestion that she may not be able to bear a child as a result of the damage done to her body when she was raped by Fascist soldiers. When Jordan and Maria make love the earth moves, but it is not a question of the union of heaven and earth in cosmogonic mythology (Melville's sky and sea joining at the horizon): the earth moves "out and away from them" and time stops—that is, lovemaking removes the pair from reality. The treatment of Maria and the love affair of Maria and Jordan is thus seen to be full of contradictions in its symbolical implications, as though Hemingway is divided between belief in the cycle of life and his own predilection for a final and issueless act of heroism. The best that can be said is that fertility imagery is used ambiguously, not ironically as it is in the final scene of *Farewell to Arms*, when Catherine dies and her child lies stillborn in a rainy season.

Pilar, moving in mystery but hardly ambiguity, is Hemingway's finest female character with the exception of Brett, whose exact opposite she is: Pilar the pro-

tective, Brett the destructive goddess. Pilar and Ma
Joad, to whom may be added Dilsey, are characters in-
corporating all the commonly ascribed traits of motherhood on a realistic level but standing forth in some
extrarealistic way as well. They are larger than life and
seem to draw on divine sources for their strong will, their
unrationalized sense of necessity, their power over the
lives of others. They do not die; they survive when
others succumb, though they passionately want others
to survive too. Pilar has "a brown face like a model for
a granite monument"; she is "something barbarous,"
can read men's fates in their palms, can even smell the
"odor of death" on doomed men. She belongs among
those women in heroic poetry who combine the activities
of the sorceress, warrior, and woman of the house.[5]
After telling the story of the death of her matador lover,
she thinks of herself, "I last. . . . Yes, I have lasted.
But for what?" One answer may be: to serve Maria, just
as Ma Joad serves Rosasharn and Dilsey serves Benjy—
to serve the innocent so that they will survive.

Criticism has often referred to *For Whom the Bell
Tolls* as an epic. Julian Hartt calls it "a novel more
nearly epic . . . than any other in our time." [6] Carlos
Baker entitles one section of his book on Hemingway
"The Epic Genre" on the ground that "the novel is a
living example of how, in modern times, the epic quality
must probably be projected." [7] Among the "elements of
the epic manner . . . successfully adapted to modern
needs," Baker lists the following:

> A primitive setting, simple food and wine, the care
> and use of weapons, the sense of imminent danger,
> the emphasis on masculine prowess, the presence of
> varying degrees of courage and cowardice, the rude
> barbarisms on both sides, the operation of certain
> religious and magical superstitions, the warrior
> codes. . . .[8]

Others are "the consciousness of the supernatural," "the intentionally heightened language," "an over-all seriousness of conception," and "the full panoply of time past . . . at work in time present." Most important is Hemingway's use of synecdoche, "the device by which a part can be made to function for the whole, and the fact to gain an emblematic power without the loss of its native particularity." What Hemingway's "synecdochist's triumph" is, precisely, Baker does not show in detail; by inference it must mean that Hemingway avoids the pitfalls of epic swelling and grandioseness by limiting his work to a realistic account of Spanish guerillas fighting a single battle just as Homer succeeds "by carefully centering his attention on the action before Troy." The action at the bridge is a synecdoche for the entire Spanish war, and the Spanish war, as it turned out (luckily for Hemingway), became a miniature preview of World War II. "No kind of adventure is so common or better told in the earlier heroic manner than the defence of a narrow place against odds," writes W. P. Ker in his study of medieval heroic poetry.[9] Hemingway's bridge is carefully kept the visual center of the action; when we are not viewing it from the surrounding slopes, we are rehearsing over and over again the plans for its destruction. Robert Jordan ends his heroic exploit just as he began it, on "the brown, pine-needled floor of the forest" within sight of the bridge. In the manner of the epic hero, Jordan entertains a very simple view of the bridge and its relations to the cause: its successful demolition will assure General Golz a successful campaign, a number of successful campaigns will defeat the Fascists, and defeating the Fascists in Spain will lead to their defeat everywhere: "If we win here we will win everywhere." The guerilla attack upon the bridge is Hemingway's graphic simplification of World War II.

Epic narrative alternates between concentration and

expansion. The bridge focuses the action narrowly; seven digressions carry the action beyond the bridge and the mountains. Of these, two are clearly related to the predicament of the hero: one is Pilar's story of the matador Finito de Palencia, who "was afraid all the time and in the ring he was like a lion"; the other is Pilar's disquisition on the ability of some gifted people, like herself, to smell "the odor of death" on those people who are about to die. We never know whether Pilar detects the fateful odor on Jordan, though she claims to have detected it on his predecessor, Kashkin. Along with her refusal to tell what she sees in Jordan's palm, the conversation about the odor of death seems to confirm Pilar's function as a prophetess. The discussion of death is also clearly marked as an important part of the education of the hero. Pilar says to Jordan: "All right, *Inglés*. Learn. That's the thing. Learn." Jordan replies, "If it is necessary for one to learn let us learn." The stories of Pablo's execution of Fascist sympathizers, of the Fascist soldiers' mistreatment of Maria and her family, and of Jordan's encounters with revolutionary leaders in Madrid broaden the account of the war, the first two by giving examples of atrocities committed in small towns and the other by lifting the curtain on intrigues at headquarters. The last digression is the journey of Andrés, a partisan entrusted to deliver Jordan's message to General Golz. The trip is presented in a series of scenes that are alternated with scenes depicting the attack on the bridge; while Andrés is delayed time and again by the stupidity of bureaucrats, Jordan is expeditiously blowing the bridge. The juxtaposition of two opposed kinds of action has a melodramatic effect, better suited to the cinema than to the novel. We recall the sentimental effect of Norris's juxtaposition of scenes at the end of *The Octupus*. Still, the sequence carries Andrés and the reader through the entire chain of command of a Loyalist army and serves to complete the variety of leaders Hemingway is so intent on studying and implicitly comparing with Jordan.

The heightening of language cited by Baker is of course a result of Hemingway's "translation" of the colloquial Spanish dialogue of his characters into an English idiom that is strangely formalized and stiff. This English-as-translation varies from normal English not markedly enough to make it bizarre but just enough to lend a special tone of epic seriousness and heroism. It succeeds in saving from bathos scenes like the final parting of the lovers and in making credible the devotion and courage of fighters like El Sordo. Although archaic and even, as one commentator claims, Elizabethan,[10] Hemingway's special stylistic effects are not laid on so thickly as to violate the realistic conventions of the novel—as Melville's do in *Moby-Dick*. It is as much Hemingway's adaptation of language as his "uses of synecdoche" that accounts for his success in "keeping the epic genre in good health," as Baker puts it, and avoiding the "false epic quality" that Hemingway himself had warned against in *Death in the Afternoon*.

"If *For Whom the Bell Tolls* is a kind of epic, it is above all a tragic epic," writes Baker. In this respect it is like other American epic novels that present a heroic adventure ending in decline and failure. At the very start of his mission Jordan is warned by General Golz, "Merely to blow the bridge is a failure," and this is precisely what happens: the Fascist forces are prepared for the attack before the bridge is even blown, but since it is too late to call off the attack Jordan must go ahead with his task even though he knows it is useless. Leading to this ultimate frustration is the familiar tragic declension, the series of unhappy accidents. On the night that El Sordo goes out to steal enough horses for the guerillas it snows and he is followed back to his stronghold and, with his entire band, wiped out by the Fascist cavalry. This disaster makes Jordan shorthanded and the chances for escape after the blowing almost nil. Then Pablo destroys the exploder and detonator. This further increases the difficulty of blowing the bridge and getting out alive. Finally, Jordan, learning that the enemy is prepared for the attack, sends to General Golz a message that arrives too late for the attack to be stopped. Although the blowing of the bridge serves no useful purpose, duty requires that it be carried out at a great loss. The guerilla band is decimated and the remnant must leave their stronghold for another of unknown suitability. Jordan is left to face the enemy alone, a certain death in store for him. His tragedy is the greatest: he has lost his mission, his love, his dearest friend, Anselmo, and he is about to give up his life. And yet he remains undiscouraged to the end: "If this attack is no good another one will be," he tells himself. In remaining behind to cover the flight of Maria and the band, he wins a victory over the fear of cowardice and the temptation to escape reality, as his father had done by suicide, or as his predecessor, Kashkin, had done by having himself killed. This final act of heroism stands in contrast to the frustration of heroic action at the close of *The Octopus* and *The Grapes of Wrath*.

Jordan has an heroic apotheosis like Roland's. As they are about to die, Roland with his sword Durendal and Jordan with his submachine gun prepare to face the enemy who, for an overwhelming reason—Christianity in the one case, antifascism in the other—must not be allowed to pass. At the point of expiring each kills his last foe: Roland breaks his horn on the skull of a paynim thief; Jordan, though the outcome is not narrated, most certainly will kill Lieutenant Berrendo as soon as he rides into range. This will be a fitting revenge, for it was Lieutenant Berrendo who led the murderous attack on

El Sordo. Each hero dies beneath a pine tree in a special and sacred place. Thus Roland

> *Far as a quarrel flies from a cross-bow drawn,*
> *Toward land of Spain he goes, to a wide lawn,*
> *And climbs a mound where grows a fair tree tall,*
> *And marble stones beneath it stand by four.*
> *Face downward there on the green grass he falls,*
> *And swoons away, for he is at death's door.*[11]

Jordan dies in a place held sacred by a succession of Hemingway heroes, a pine grove bordering a meadow. This is where the youngster Nick Adams had his first sexual experience ("Fathers and Sons"), where an older Nick Adams returns to soothe his war-torn nerves ("Big Two-Hearted River: Part 1"), where Lieutenant Henry and Catherine loved to walk when they lived in Switzerland, and where Jordan himself first observed the bridge at the start of his mission. The most important love and war experiences of the hero occur in this spot. For Nick the place is curative:

> Around the grove of trees was a bare space. It was brown and soft underfoot as Nick walked on it. This was the over-lapping of the pine needle floor, extending out beyond the width of the high branches. The trees had grown tall and the branches moved high, leaving in the sun this bare space they had once covered with shadow. Sharp at the edge of this extension of the forest floor commenced the sweet fern.
>
> Nick slipped off his pack and lay down in the shade. He lay on his back and looked up into the pine trees. His neck and the small of his back rested as he stretched. The earth felt good against his back. He looked up at the sky, through the branches, and then shut his eyes. He opened them and looked up again.

There was a wind high up in the branches. He shut his eyes again and went to sleep.[12]

For Jordan it is the place of death:

And he lay very quietly and tried to hold on to himself. . . . He was completely integrated now and he took a good long look at everything. Then he looked up at the sky. There were big white clouds in it. He touched the palm of his hand against the pine needles where he lay and he touched the bark of the pine trunk that he lay behind. . . . He was waiting until the officer reached the sunlit place where the first trees of the pine forest joined the green slope of the meadow. He could feel his heart beating against the pine needle floor of the forest.[13]

The two widely separated scenes present no irony even though one young man lies down to sleep and the other to kill and to die, for each feels reassured by being in touch with the reality of earth, tree, and sky; and each is at the "sunlit place" where pine woods join the meadow, the inner sanctum of Hemingway's sacred spot where life and death meet in mysterious union.

In *The Sun Also Rises*, Jake Barnes and Bill Gorton end their week of fishing by walking up the mountain to the monastery at Roncesvalles. "It's a remarkable place," says Harris, the Englishman who has accompanied them on their fishing trips. Bill's reaction to this is, "It isn't the same as fishing, though, is it?" It is to these same mountains that the Hemingway hero returns many years later, not to fish but to fight and die in a crusade—like Roland at Roncesvalles. The hero returns to war and social commitment. In *Farewell to Arms* he had given up his occupation as soldier and had sought an escape in the love of woman. This failed him and he was left with nothing, neither love nor heroism. Now, in

For Whom the Bell Tolls, he has resumed his occupation; his prowess is unimpeachable, and he dies
bravely, honoring both himself and mankind. While
Lieutenant Henry's romance with Catherine leads
eventually to her death, Jordan is directly responsible
for Maria's rescue from death. Instead of being destroyed
by war and woman, as Jake Barnes is in *The Sun Also
Rises*, Jordan is a hero apotheosized through sacrificing
himself for the innocent woman and distinguishing
himself in war. Jordan participates, not in a fiasco of
war like the retreat at Caporetto, but in a common en-
deavor having transcendent consequences in spite of its
ironical aspects.

Only once in his career, however, does Hemingway so
happily combine personal honor and social responsibility,
gross and innocent love, violence and transcendence.
When we see the hero in war a third time, he has
become sadly diminished, for just as *For Whom the
Bell Tolls* is a reaction against *Farewell to Arms*, so
Across the River and into the Trees reacts bitterly
against *For Whom the Bell Tolls*. Colonel Cantwell,
the Hemingway hero grown old in the battles of his
country, has seen so much more of war than Robert
Jordan that he cannot accept his part in it with anything but bitterness and disgust. Yet, being a professional soldier and still retaining some faith in the
cause of democratic arms, he cannot bring himself to
make a separate peace, as Lieutenant Henry so easily
did before him, even though he too has a romantic
interest to distract him. Thus Colonel Cantwell stands
somwehere between the changeableness of Lieutenant
Henry and the steadfastness of Robert Jordan. Lieutenant Henry found both love and war to be meaning-
less; Jordan experiences both love and glory in war.
Cantwell is willing to grant that "it is only what man
does for woman that he retains, except what he does

for his fatherland," that love is "the only mystery that he believed in except the occasional bravery of man." But there is no luster for him in either love or war because he has been so deeply immersed in the corruption and stupidity of life. The whole novel is taken up with his effort to purge himself of the taint of having lived so long by reviewing his past in the presence of his young Italian sweetheart, significantly named Renata. Like Desdemona, the Venetian princess listens hour after hour to a recital, not of the glories of a lifetime spent in war, but of the bloody and stupid conduct of war. Renata thinks of the purgation of Cantwell's bitterness as a preparation for his death: "Don't you know I want you to die with the grace of a happy death?" But the Colonel's mind and body cannot be made well, as his name suggests; nor can he hope to experience a rebirth, as Renata's name promises. In a portrait painted by one of her friends, Renata is made to look as though she is "rising from the sea without the hair wet," an obvious reference to Botticelli's Birth of Venus. Renata makes fun of this detail and presents the portrait to Cantwell, who later carries on a drunken conversation with it in her absence. Clearly, Renata cannot bring her lover to a rebirth, as Catherine does for Lieutenant Henry, or to a heroic sacrifice, as Maria does for Robert Jordan. After an unsuccessful duck hunt and unsatisfying love-tryst, Colonel Cantwell dies in the back seat of his car.

Across the River and into the Trees is a travesty of all that Hemingway had glorified in For Whom the Bell Tolls. Love is a playful interlude with an ineffectual Venus, at best a sad therapy easing death. Death is demeaned and heroism in war is hedged about with ugly circumstances. The scene in which Cantwell announces to Renata his imminent death reads like a parody of the lovers' farewell in the earlier book. The Colonel says he wants to be buried "Up in the hills. . . . On any part of the high ground where we beat them." This sounds like Roland again, but the mood rapidly changes. The girl not too enthusiastically replies:

"I will go with you if you like."
"I would not like. That is the one thing we do alone. Like going to the bathroom. . . . No. You get married and have five sons and call them all Richard."
"The lion-hearted," the girl said. . . .
"The crap-hearted," the Colonel said.[14]

The community of noble partisans is parodied in the Order, a private joke between Colonel Cantwell and the headwaiter of the Hotel Gritti, where the Colonel does much of his heavy drinking. The Order, *El Ordine Militar, Nobile y Espirituoso de los Caballeros de Brusadelli*, is "named after a particularly notorious multi-millionaire non-taxpaying profiteer of Milan, who had, in the course of a dispute over property, accused his young wife, publicly and legally through due process of law, of having deprived him of his judgment through her extraordinary sexual demands" (pp. 56–57). The noble and heroic Spanish of the former novel is now "the best language for founding orders." The wound Cantwell had received in World War I is also debased when he defecates on the spot at Fossalta where he received it. The place is the same where Nick Adams and Lieutenant Henry were wounded in the war: on the bank of a slow and muddy river as it bends through a swamp. "The fishing would be tragic there" for Nick in "Big Two-Hearted River." It is a terrain the Colonel has "strange dreams" about, and it haunts Nick when he is having his bad time in the bunk at Captain Paravicini's dugout in "A Way You'll Never Be." Hemingway's language of places becomes clear when we recall that Robert Jordan is shot in a mountain pass and lies wounded in a sacred place from where he can see the bridge and the fast-running river far below.

It is possible to interpret Hemingway's three American war heroes as reflections of the changing role of the United States in European wars of the twentieth century. Lieutenant Henry could then be taken to represent the partial commitment of American forces in World War I; Jordan the total commitment, even to the point of cooperating with Communist allies, at the height of World War II; and Colonel Cantwell the growing disillusionment with Cold War politics. *For Whom the Bell Tolls* is obviously a more conscious expression of the times than the other two, more personally oriented, novels. The battle epic was a need of the 1930s which prompted Steinbeck to write an epic novel of economic strife and Hemingway an epic novel of war. For the occasion Hemingway adapted the epic as a means of dealing with the approaching world holocaust and placing his lifetime hero in the stream of history. The result is a successful compromise between epic tradition and the author's deeper commitment to a purely personal form of heroism.

The lonely, isolated heroism of the defeated man is restored, and indeed raised to a metaphysical level of symbolism, in *The Old Man and the Sea*. Santiago is Robert Jordan removed from history and the folly of war and politics, from the brotherhood of warriors, cleansed of romantic passion, and stripped of the civilized complexities that filled Jordan's life with doubt and dismay. His dreams are singularly placid:

> He no longer dreamed of storms, nor of women, nor of great occurrences, nor of great fish, nor fights, nor contests of strength, nor of his wife. He only dreamed of places now and of the lions on the beach. They played like young cats in the dusk and he loved them as he loved the boy.[15]

All that is left is the hero's prowess and determination, the simple tools and weapons of the chase, and the quarry, a monster which is yet his "brother." Santiago wins and loses, like Jordan, but all is starkly clear in a universe consisting of sea, sky, and shore. Only one human relationship exists for the old man: the boy who sometimes helps him with his fishing has become like a son to him. Jordan regretted that he had no one to whom he could pass on what he had learned in his brief heroic hour, and his own model hero was his grandfather, not his father. In *The Old Man and the Sea* Hemingway ends his long series of father-son failures with a relationship that is as nearly perfect as it can be in an imperfect world: Manolin is the beneficiary of Santiago's heroism although Manolin is another man's son. Hemingway cherished the relationship of hero-father to son more than the relationship of epic hero to society, the isolated more than the public act of heroism. Like Norris before him, he finally rejected the idea of heroism in war, the idea of the *Iliad* epic.

5

Bellow's Odysseys

The last four novels of Saul Bellow are devoted to a single theme: the effort of a perplexed man to discover enough of himself and reality to continue living in a time of personal and public crisis. Introspection, or the nervous exercise of a contemporary consciousness, is the means of discovery for the disturbed hero and forms the substance of the novels. To supply a narrative ground for the intellectualization and verbalization of his introverted characters, Bellow uses the metaphor of the journey of the man of many troubles, Odysseus. Each of his heroes finds himself alienated from father, wife, and children and undertakes a journey of return in the course of which he experiences death and learns important philosophical lessons. The amounts of introspective and narrative materials vary from novel to novel: in *The Adventures of Augie March*, a work anticipating the form and theme of the subsequent four novels, the proportion of action to introspection is high, in *Seize the Day* and *Herzog* it is quite low, in *Henderson the Rain King* and *Mr. Sammler's Planet* a perfect balance is struck. The age of Bellow's Odyssean figure ranges from early middle-age in *Henderson* to "seventy-plus" in *Mr. Sammler's Planet,* and the gounds of his perplexity remain about the same. It is the development of different kinds of introspection and the astonishing variety of the journey devised for each new wanderer that

is the measure of Bellow's genius and the constant
delight of his readers.

In *Seize the Day* the story gets no further than the
breakdown of the man of troubles in a fit of weeping
as he stands over the coffin of a complete stranger:

> The source of all tears had suddenly sprung open
> within him, black, deep, and hot. . . . The great knot
> of ill and grief in his throat swelled upward and he
> gave in utterly and held his face and wept. He cried
> with all his heart. . . .
>
> The flowers and lights fused ecstatically in Wil-
> helm's blind, wet eyes; the heavy sea-like music came
> up to his ears. It poured into him where he had hidden
> himself in the center of a crowd by the great and
> happy oblivion of tears. He heard it and sank deeper
> than sorrow, through torn sobs and cries toward
> the consummation of his heart's ultimate need.[1]

Ihab Hassan selects this passage for special attention,
remarking on the suddenness with which Bellow moves
from "worldly terms" to "a more exalted level of per-
ception."[2] Perhaps it is the veiled parallel with the
plight of Odysseus, particularly as he wept on the shore
of Ogygia, that helps to create the tone remarked by
Hassan. There is nothing sudden or unique about this
passage, however—there are others like it—nor, in the
light of the Odyssean parallel, is there a resolution in
Wilhelm's weeping. He ends only where Odysseus
began, and we cannot imagine for him a victorious
return and settlement of his problems. His surrogate
father, Dr. Tamkin, has given him valuable advice—to
concentrate on *being* rather than *becoming*—and while
this may be the truth that Wilhelm needs to restore his
life, it comes from a man whose dishonesty, selfishness,
and flippant manner inspire distrust. To be saved Wilhelm needs love, which his real father, Dr. Adler, re-

fuses to give him because he cannot conceive that his
son wants anything but money from him. Dr. Adler, a
prominent and respected man, refuses to "carry" his
son, whom he considers a weakling, a "slob." He fails
like the eagle in *The Adventures of Augie March.*

Tommy's final break with his father occurs in a scene
that makes an interesting variation of the descent into
the underworld and contributes, along with the weeping
scene already cited, to the mystery and elevation of tone
remarked by Hassan. Desperately seeking his father in
the hour of his greatest need, Tommy telephones the
massage room of the hotel where his father lives. The
attendant there, "the old Czech prizefighter with the
deformed nose and ears," answers the call but does not
return with Dr. Adler. "A hollow endless silence
followed." After fortifying himself with a Phenaphen
pill, Tommy takes the elevator

> down to the health club. Through the steamy
> windows, when he emerged, he saw the reflection of
> the swimming pool swirling green at the bottom of
> the lowest stairway. . . . Wilhelm descended to the
> massage room. On the tables naked men were lying.
> It was not a brightly lighted place, and it was very
> hot, and under the white faint moons of the ceiling
> shone pale skins. . . . Dr. Adler was on the fourth
> table, and Wilhelm stood over his father's pale, slight
> body. (Pp. 107–8)

Dr. Adler refuses to say the "one word" that Tommy
requires and dismisses his son with "Go away from me
now. It's torture for me to look at you, you slob!" The
father denies his son love, but Tommy cannot withhold
his love even from strangers no matter how despicable
they are. This discovery is made in another descent
scene in an "underground corridor" beneath Times
Square; there "in the dark tunnel, in the haste, heat, and

darkness which disfigure and make freaks and fragments of nose and eyes and teeth, all of a sudden, unsought, a general love for all these imperfect and lurid-looking people burst out in Wilhelm's breast" (pp. 84–85). At the time he was skeptical of this "onrush of loving kindness" and dismissed it as "only another one of those subway things"; but the love of mankind comes over him again, more dramatically and mixed now with self-pity, in the final scene on his "day of reckoning" when by mistake he falls in with a funeral procession and eventually finds himself looking down at the expression on the face of the deceased and breaking into tears. Thus, although there are three encounters with the dead in the experience of Tommy Wilhelm, his quest ends inconclusively. Augie March, we recall, is last seen laughing uncontrollably at a poor French girl when she avers, "Ah, the dream of my life is to go to Mexico!" But the laughing, he speculates, may not be directed against her but "at nature—including eternity—that it thinks it can win over us and the power of hope." Augie thus comes finally to a hopeful acceptance of the absurdities and ambiguities of life. In Tommy Wilhelm's profound recognition of the pain and trouble of life the Bellow hero is carried one step further, but it remains for Henderson and Herzog to win victories over their troubles and complete the form of the Odyssean epic.

The next two variations of Bellow's favorite theme make a pair of complementary odysseys, *Henderson the Rain King* being the more traditional journey of the hero to resolve his problems through a series of unusual exploits and *Herzog* being the more contemporary adaptation in which thought and interiorization play a greater role than action. Henderson is a serio-comic Odysseus reveling in flamboyant gestures and extravagant boasts, while Herzog is a self-effacing traveler of the mind, "Odysseus, Flat on His Back," as one critic aptly calls him in the title of his review.[3] *Henderson* is so packed with incident that it is difficult to disentangle the Odyssean motifs from the stories of many other literary prototypes—Gawain, Don Quixote, Gargantua, Twain's Connecticut Yankee, Francis Macomber, and, indeed, Macomber's creator, Ernest Hemingway. On the other hand, *Herzog* has such a wealth of introspective material that the basic narrative line is concealed, but there is only one, the Odyssean.

Herzog shares with Joyce's *Ulysses* the technique of attaching an exhaustively detailed contemporary consciousness to the broad outline of an ancient narrative. The inner thought of Moses Herzog (a name borrowed from the Cyclops chapter in *Ulysses*) is conveyed both by the stream of consciousness of the subject character and the traditional objective point of view of the author; his outer, more rhetorical thought is rendered by the old device of placing into the record the letters he writes to a broad assortment of friends and public figures, living and dead. The narrative is made up of ingredients that reflect the story of Odysseus: the forlorn wanderer who returns from his travels to learn that he has lost his rightful place at home and sets about restoring himself. Despite his sedentary occupation—he is a professor— and his penchant for thought, Herzog travels extensively in the course of his lifetime and in the few days that he is revealed to us in the novel. At the beginning of the novel he is seen returning from Europe, where he had gone on his doctor's advice when his second marriage started to fail. "Half buttoned, red-eyed, unshaved," he seemed to himself "to be a broken-down monarch of some kind." Instead of going directly to his family in Chicago he stops in New York and learns from his Aunt Zelda what the situation at home is: his wife is now living openly with his rival, a man named Gersbach, and wants a divorce. For five days he postpones acting on this information. He travels to Martha's Vineyard and immediately returns, he visits a lady friend and is tempted to go off with her. Ramona is described as a "sexual priestess" who excels in supplying sensual gratification of the most sophisticated sort. She is eager to have Herzog live with her at her house in Montauk, Long Island:

> Never idle, his mind's eye saw Montauk—white beaches, flashing light, glossy breakers, horseshoe crabs perishing in their armor, sea robins and blowfish. Herzog longed to lie down in his bathing trunks, and warm his troubled belly on the sand. But how could he? To accept too many favors from Ramona was dangerous. He might have to pay with his freedom.[4]

He compromises by spending a night with Ramona in her lavish West Side apartment, which is decorated with "Moorish knickknacks and arabesques" and from which New York harbor can be seen. It is a night of luxurious dining and lovemaking. To Ramona Herzog, "against his will," tells his sad story—"how he was swindled, conned, manipulated, his savings taken, driven into debt, his trust betrayed by wife, friend, physician"—and she responds by offering him love: "She transformed his miseries into sexual excitements and, to give credit where it was due, turned his grief in a useful direction." Her effort "to renew the spirit through the flesh" Herzog recognizes as a danger: "This—this asylum was his for the asking, he believed. Then why didn't he ask? Because today's asylum might be the dungeon of tomorrow."

Having successfully resisted Ramona's temptation, Herzog goes to confront his wife and her lover in Chicago where they are now living together. First, however, he equips himself with a pistol that he takes from "his late father's house," where his stepmother still lives. The scene at her house gets its narrative power from the same combination of death and alienation that characterizes the massage room scene in *Seize the Day*. "Face white, mouth grim, he mounted the stairs in the shadow of approaching sunset, and pressed the button." Tante Taube, his "ancient step-mother," opens the door after long delay—"what a face he saw, how grooved with woe and age, lined downward at the mouth!" To his question concerning her health she replies: "You see. The living dead." They sit in "the faint twilit parlor," where he breathes "the old spice, the dark, heavy air" and recalls memories of the past, including the assault his father made upon him when he returned once to the home, the prodigal son, and threw himself on his father's mercy, "with that Christianized smirk of the long-suffering son." From its hiding place Herzog takes the pistol that his father had threatened him with. As he leaves the house Taube warns him, "You got a lot of trouble? Don't make it worser, Moshe."

An earlier scene, in a subway, is a more specific descent into the underworld very much like Tommy Wilhelm's "underground corridor" experience. It occurs when Herzog is on the way to Ramona's apartment. Just before descending the subway steps at sunset he watches a demolition crew burning the debris from a wrecked building, "the funeral of exhausted objects." In the light of the setting sun "Herzog observed that the people were spattered with red stains, and that he himself was flecked on the arms and chest. He crossed Seventh Avenue and entered the subway." In the subway station he sees the same "slogans and exhortations" on the walls, the same disfigurements of human forms, and is struck with the same sentimental feeling for mankind that moved Tommy. It occurs to him that "innumerable millions of passengers had polished the wood of the turnstile with their hips. From this arose a feeling of communion." Herzog is even more critical than Tommy of such feelings, which he calls "potato love," but they operate upon him nonetheless, as they do upon Tommy, and contribute to the eventual resolution of his troubles.

Fully aroused by the situation at home and armed with a weapon, Herzog finally proceeds to his home in Chicago and spies upon his wife and her lover; but when he sees his rival bathing his daughter, in a setting of perfect domestic tranquillity, he abandons any thought he had of revenge and hastily retreats. "Firing his pistol was nothing but a thought," anyway. Ironically, he is soon after this arrested for carrying a dangerous weapon, and he spends a harrowing day in court and lockup, a kind of inferno where he is thrown together with people worse off than he is. In these premises Herzog feels himself to be a sort of Dante: "This . . . was not the sphere of *his* sins. He was merely passing through." Madeleine, his wife, comes, not to redeem him as Beatrice, but to accuse: her eyes "expressed a total will that he should die."

Herzog's true return, it develops, is not to the Chicago house occupied by his wife but to the home he and his wife had established in the Berkshires when they were first married. It is to this house that Herzog makes his way alone. He begins restoring the house, which has fallen into disrepair during his absence, and making it suitable for living. There he rests and recovers his composure: "Whatever had come over him during these last months, the spell, really seemed to be passing, really going." He hires a woman to help him clean up the house, and his last thought is to "tell her to sprinkle the floor."

Such is the simple action of the book, and although it covers an actual period of no more than a week, considerably more action is presented through Herzog's reminiscences, which, operating like Homer's flashbacks, present the whole of Herzog's life. Though Herzog's experiences are no match for Odysseus's wondrous adventures, they have a breadth that is in keeping with epic practice. He has traveled extensively, seen many lands, known many people, including women of many nationalities—his two wives (Jewish-American), Sono (Japanese), Wanda (Polish), and Ramona (French-Russian-Argentine-Jewish). His intellect has ranged over a wide variety of subjects—philosophical, political, moral, literary, scientific—and times. Through his letters he "speaks" with many notables the world over, both living and dead; he uses many languages—Latin, French, German, Italian, Yiddish, Hebrew—and scours his memory for proverbs, quotations, and songs. The total effect is encyclopedic, a mingling of many subjects and styles that is characteristic of the epic.

The quest of this latter-day Odysseus is to find a reason for living as well as a home and family to return to. The very first note Herzog jots down during the period of his travail reads: *"Death—die—live again—die again—live."* The existential question is not only for himself but for all: *"People are dying—it is no metaphor—for lack of something real to carry home when day is done."* His private struggle to find a way through his troubles, his "ordinary existence," is, he insists, of "historic importance." In aggrandizing his theme by making Herzog representative of man of his time and of the issues he faces, the author places his work in the epic class. The *Odyssey* was Homer's extraordinary exploration of private virtue in his time, as the *Iliad* was his presentation of more conventional public virtues. The lesson Herzog learns is for his times as well as for himself: by extricating himself from his difficulties he helps to disprove the fashionable idea "that this is a doomed time, that we are waiting for the end."

Through obstacles and temptations Herzog makes his way home, but not in the manner of a mighty warrior overcoming great physical odds. Herzog's is a spiritual victory made possible by arduous thinking on his problems, facing them incessantly from every angle, pondering his life in relation to the lives of others. Like the long-suffering Odysseus, he learns that his afflictions must not immobilize him and monopolize his life, that their recital to friends and strangers is a fatal corruption; he finally rejects the temptation—a modern fashion—to make of his woes a "doctrine or theology of suffering. . . . I will never expound suffering for anyone or call for Hell to make us serious and truthful." Self-love avoided, he must steer a course between hatred and sentimental love for others. These are two perils represented by Herzog's two lawyer friends, Simkin in New York and Sandor Himmelstein in Chicago. Simkin, a suave sybarite, advises Herzog to get revenge for the wrongs done to him by bringing Madeleine and Gersbach to court, demanding custody of the child, and subjecting the pair to scandalous publicity. Simkin stirs in his client an "eccentric, dangerous force," which is felt with alarming keenness as Herzog watches several court trials—"That force of balked longing coming back as stinging poison." Although the destruction Herzog risks with Himmelstein comes to us in a flashback, it is more terrifying than Simkin's threat. Himmelstein is portrayed as a monster, a "fierce dwarf with protruding teeth" and "hellish tongue." He, too, is poisonous—"a fierce green, milky poison rose to his eyes"—and frightens Herzog. Ironically, the misshapen Himmelstein offers not hate, but love, a perverted variety of "potato love": he makes homosexual advances to Herzog. Herzog escapes and the horrible recollection of his stay in Himmelstein's apartment is followed by a beautiful passage on the sea, to which Herzog returns again and again for consolation.

In the mild end of the afternoon, later, at the waterside in Woods Hole, waiting for the ferry, he looked through the green darkness at the net of bright reflections on the bottom. He loved to think about the power of the sun, about light, about the ocean. The purity of the air moved him. There was no stain in the water, where schools of minnows swam. Herzog sighed and said to himself, "Praise God—praise God." His breathing had become freer. His heart was greatly stirred by the open horizon; the deep colors; the faint iodine pungency of the Atlantic rising from weeds and mollusks; the white, fine, heavy sand; but principally by the green transparency as he looked down to the stony bottom webbed with golden lines. (P. 91)

For all its emphasis upon thought, *Herzog* has great narrative moments supported by descriptions of lyric beauty.

The struggle of Herzog is for the restoration of his sanity, and this is accomplished by purging himself of self-pity, on the one hand, and of bitterness against man and God for his troubles, on the other. The book begins with the statement "If I am out of my mind, it's all right with me," but this reflects a defensive attitude and is belied by the earnest intellectual struggle of Herzog throughout his ordeal to preserve his sanity. "How my mind has struggled to make coherent sense," he writes to God in the last letter. In spite of buffetings, like Odysseus he retains his piety and his piety underlies reason; skepticism, "accusing God of murder," leads to "the victory of death, not of rationality, not of rational faith." Herzog succeeds in making his peace with men as well as with God when he realizes that "the real and essential question is one of our employment by other human beings and their employment by us. Without this true employment you never dread death, you cultivate it." Thus, though he performs nothing heroic, Herzog escapes death and wins through to a conception of himself that is not unheroic, and the end of the book finds him eager to be up and doing—"A loving brute—a subtle, spoiled, loving man. Who can make use of him? He craves use."

He has not had to settle accounts with his wife and her lover, as justice and the old tradition of revenge required, because he has deemed it better to accept the evil done to him. This in no way decreases our respect for him, for he has avoided easy and violent solutions and has fought a sensitive spiritual battle, and, in the physical sense, has actually recovered a home for himself and even plans to have his son join him there.

While settling himself in his Berkshire home, Herzog gets the idea to write "an Insect Iliad" for his daughter Junie:

> He could make the Trojans ants. The Argives might be water-skaters . . . with long velvet hairs beaded with glittering oxygen. Helen, a beautiful wasp. Old Priam a cicada, sucking sap from the roots and with his trowel-shaped belly plastering the tunnels. And Achilles a stag-beetle with sharp spikes and terrible strength, but doomed to a brief life though half a god. At the edge of the water he cried out to his mother
>
> > *Thus spoke Achilles*
> > *And Thetis heard him in the ooze,*
> > *Sitting beside her ancient father*
> > *In glorious debris, enough for all.*
> >   (Pp. 324–25)

Herzog is full of "this heartfelt nonsense," but in his present excited state he cannot control his imagination for an extended literary effort and the project is abandoned. He returns instead to painting a piano, which he intends to ship to Junie in Chicago. This project, too, is proved by his brother to be quite impractical. The idea for the "Insect Iliad" has precedent, of course, in Thoreau's mock-epic Battle of the Ants in *Walden* (part of the chapter "Brute Neighbors") and ultimately in the ancient parody of the *Iliad*, the *Batrachomyomachia*. Nor is it inappropriate for the Odyssean hero to view as extravagant the heroics of the *Iliad* since Odysseus must solve a messy domestic problem with methods that are hardly those of the field of battle. However, Herzog's notes, with their tender regard for Homeric characters, do not seem to describe a mock-epic. It is, after all, to be a gift for Junie, whose pleasure in it he anticipates; and the scene between Achilles and Thetis is sympathetically echoed on the next page when Herzog imagines calling upon his mother:

> *The life you gave me has been curious,* he wanted to say to his mother, *and perhaps the death I must inherit will turn out to be even more profoundly curious. I have sometimes wished it would hurry up, longed for it to come soon. But I am still on the same side of eternity as ever. It's just as well, for I have certain things still to do.* (P. 326)

The absurd, the ridiculous, the laughable in his own predicament are never overlooked by the scrupulously honest hero of *Herzog*, but they never interrupt for long the solemn tone of the book.

It is rather in *Henderson the Rain King* that comedy will be found to have its full play, and to such an extent that early reviewers could see nothing but fun and nonsense in the book. True, Henderson's absurd predicaments, madcap behavior, and foolish chatter place him in the company of Don Quixote, Gargantua, and Twain's Hank Morgan; but underneath these appearances there is the sorely afflicted Odysseus. The America pictured in *Henderson* is a long way from the all-too-solid New York and Chicago that press so heavily on Tommy

Wilhelm and Herzog, but it is only Henderson's playful distortions that make it seem so distant, and under the surrealistic surface are the easily discernible features of reality. Henderson's journey takes him to places "beyond geography," to an Africa as fantastic as Homer's Mediterranean countries, and yet the beliefs and customs he reports are real enough anthropologically, being drawn from such authorities as Frazer, Herskovits, Seligman, Speke, and Burton.[5] Bellow offends some readers because he selects the most bizarre items in the life of Africans, but these, as we shall see, are suited to his narrative purpose. Setting a cocky and gabby millionaire from Connecticut in the midst of primitive folkways is a source of humor just as surely as setting a Connecticut mechanic in the midst of medieval history. In both *Henderson* and *A Connecticut Yankee in King Arthur's Court*, a good deal of the fun depends upon the intruder's use of a casual modern colloquial style in situations still possessing, for everyone else, the solemnity of honored custom. Here is how Henderson tries to extricate himself from further involvement with affairs in the court of an African king:

> "All this couldn't be more memorable, but I don't want to outstay my welcome. I know you are planning to make rain today and probably I will only be in the way. So thanks for the hospitality of the palace, and I wish you all kinds of luck with the ceremony, but I think after lunch my man and I had better blow." [6]

Bellow mixes fantasy and realism instead of separating them as Homer does in the *Odyssey*. His fantasy world has a rational basis in anthropological data which is selected to give his hero an appropriate setting for his initiation.

"A millionaire wanderer and wayfarer," Eugene Henderson flees "his own country, settled by his forefathers," and sets out upon a quest to end the frustrations of his life and find something worth returning home to live for. The people among whom he travels take him to be a divine hero, and he is in fact a man of Gargantuan proportions. His neck size is twenty-two, his height six-feet-four, his weight two hundred and thirty pounds. His mouth is an "enormous moat," his nose so big that he can "smell the whole world." His face is like Grand Central Station and "like the clang of a bell" in expressing his feelings: "Whole crowds of them, especially the bad ones, wave to the world from the galleries of my face." When he reads a book, a good sentence turns his "brain into a volcano . . . and a regular lava of thought pours down his sides." During World War II he "held up a ruined bridge in Italy and kept it from collapsing until the engineers arrived." Many of the other characters in the book are on a comparable scale. His wife Lily is a large woman: "Two plank steaks and six bottles of beer are not too much for her when she's in condition" and in a transoceanic telephone conversation with her "the waves of half the world, the air, the water, the earth's vascular system, came in between." An African princess who admires our hero "was so heavy that her skin had turned pink from the expansion."

Henderson comes from a family distinguished by a "service ideal" and the profession of arms: "All my people have been soldiers. They protected the peasants, and they went on the crusades and fought the Mohammedans." He shares the knight errantry ideals of his ancestors: "There is some kind of service motivation which keeps on after me. . . . I would have liked to go on errands of mercy." His heroic energy is a national as well as a family trait: "Millions of Americans have gone forth since the war to redeem the present and discover the future. . . . And it's the destiny of my generation of

Americans to go out in the world and try to find the wisdom of life." Having no lack of ambition, Henderson has the problem of finding the proper outlet for it. Post–World War II America hardly seems the place for the kind of adventures proper for a hero of Henderson's magnitude, and so his author creates for him a simplified world consisting of primitive folkways and simple social organizations as an arena for his heroic exploits. Symbolic of the change in his environment are the animals he deals with: in America he raised pigs, in Africa he faces lions. Like epic heroes before him, Henderson is very much involved with animals.[7]

The removal of the hero to Africa must not be interpreted solely as a primitivist attack upon American civilization of the sort that is implicit in the works of Hemingway; it may also be seen as a motif in the tradition of the quest epic, a device to accentuate the hero's exploits by having them occur in strange lands and amid unusual circumstances. Africa admirably serves this purpose in *Henderson the Rain King*. The Amazon jungle makes another equally appropriate setting for the adventures of Lewis Moon, the hero of Peter Matthiessen's *At Play in the Fields of the Lord* (1965), who survives primitive experiences and comes out of the jungle a new man. The foreign travels of Henderson and Moon also reflect the tremendous increase of Americans who went abroad to participate in various aid programs in the years following World War II. Henderson is told by the African king who befriends him, "I knew that you went out from home in America because of a privation of high conduct." Home is not the place for heroics either for the Hemingway or Bellow hero. Henderson is uncomfortable even as a hero abroad. Such a reminder of civilization as the broken English of an African native is enough to dash the spirit of heroism in the new American candidate for honor. This would not have had the same effect on the more confident ancient world-beater, Henderson reflects: "The Romans weren't surprised, I don't think, when some Parthian or Numidian started to speak to them in Latin; they probably took it for granted." The implication is that the American is still a little shy in assuming the heroic role he must hereafter play in the world.

Like the *Odyssey*, *Henderson the Rain King* consists of two distinct chains of action which endanger the hero, a complication of affairs at home and a loosely strung series of adventures abroad. Since Henderson is first seen amid the troubles of his home situation, it appears that he is a Dantean or Tennysonian Odysseus who sets out on a second journey after his return from war and his disillusionment with life at home. He had distinguished himself in World War II, miraculously surviving the Battle of Monte Cassino; after his return he is divorced, marries a second time, and begins to find fault with his family and the life he is leading. "Family life with Lily," he confides, "was not all that might have been predicted by an optimist." His son disgusts him, "with his crew-cut hair, his hipless trunk, his button-down collar and Princeton tie, his white shoes— his practically faceless face." He fails to establish a contact with his dead father, whom he tries to reach by playing the violin in the basement of his house. But the time and the place were not right: "Clutching the neck of the little instrument as if there were strangulation in my heart, I got cramps in my neck and shoulders." In order to find his true father and the secret that will deliver him from "the body of this death," the hero must go on a journey across the sea.

Lily and Frances, his first two wives, are less like Penelope than Circe and Calypso, keeping the hero "captive" for eight years before he can depart on his trip. In this time he takes up pig farming and surrenders himself to lust and despair. At his love trysts with Lily,

he appears "in pigskin gloves and pigskin shoes, a pigskin wallet in my pocket, seething with lust and seething
with trouble." Henderson's trouble or despair is a
"disturbance" in his heart, "a voice that spoke there
and said, *I want, I want, I want.*" [8] He "would cry" and
threaten suicide, until finally, on a "day of tears and
madness," a family servant, Miss Lenox, suffers a fatal
heart attack as she overhears Henderson in a quarrel
with his wife at the breakfast table. He later discovers
the body in the kitchen and leaves a note pinned to it:
"Do not disturb." The deceased had a catalpa tree in her
yard, "of which the trunk and lower limbs were painted
light blue. She had fixed little mirrors up there, and old
bicycle lights which shone in the dark, and in summer
she liked to climb up there and sit with her cats, drinking
a can of beer." Miss Lenox is Henderson's Elpenor; it
is her death that marks the end of his eight-year captivity
and sends him on his quest. The first part of the book
ends thus: "So Miss Lenox went to the cemetery, and I
went to Idlewild and took a plane."

Henderson's Africa is the inland country to which
Odysseus was fated to travel, according to Teiresias.
There Henderson successfully passes various trials and
learns the many necessary things he could not learn at
home. To guide him, Henderson hires a native African,
Romilayu, a cross between Sancho Panza and Queequeg.
Like Don Quixote, Henderson promises to reward his
companion handsomely for his services: "knowing how
attached he was to the jeep, I told him I would give it to
him if he would take me far enough." Like Sancho,
Romilayu usually acts to restrain his heroically inclined
master. His appearance and his strange religious practices
also remind us of Queequeg.

> Old tribal scars were cut into his cheeks and his ears
> had been mutilated to look like hackles so that the
> points stuck into his hair. His nose was fine-looking

and Abyssinian, not flat. The scars and mutilations showed that he had been born a pagan, but somewhere along the way he had been converted, and now he said his prayers every evening. On his knees, he pressed his purple hands together under his chin, which receded, and with his lips pushed forward and the powerful though short muscles jumping under the skin of his arms, he'd pray. (Pp. 45–46)

Romilayu is Henderson's practical link with the primitive past. In their last experience together in Africa, Romilayu helps Henderson escape from the tomb in which they are imprisoned and is responsible for their survival in the jungle as they make their way back to life and to civilization. One recalls Ishmael's escape from drowning by means of Queequeg's coffin turned life buoy. Both Romilayu and Queequeg have the function of helping to deliver modern man from the vexations of the civilized spirit by making primitive experiences available to him. "I am an Ishmael too" and "was cast off," says Henderson. His tale tells how he avoided melancholy and suicide by going on a journey. Melville's Ishmael took to the sea as "a substitute for pistol and ball." In response to Romilayu's wish to end their journey, Henderson says, "I might as well take this .375 and blow my brains out as go home." Africa is Henderson's seven seas, a lion his white whale. "I took off for Africa, hoping to find a remedy for my situation," says Henderson, and, as a result of his journey, he found that "the world which I thought so mighty an oppressor has removed its wrath from me." Odysseus, Ishmael, and Henderson are heroes who feel the world's anger, go on a voyage to strange lands, risk their lives in perilous adventures with awful animals, "lose" their lives or identities, and finally are reborn in the real world with the strength to face its worst evils.

Henderson, just as his illustrious forebears, goes "far,

far out," beyond even the customary safari country in Africa:

> it was all simplified and splendid, and I felt I was entering the past—the real past, no history or junk like that. The prehuman past. And I believed there was something between the stones and me. The mountains were naked, and often snakelike in their forms, without trees, and you could see the clouds being born on the slopes. From this rock came vapor, but it was not like ordinary vapor, it cast a brilliant shadow. (P. 46)

After days of walking across the barren land, the hero comes to the village of the Arnewi, a village "older than the city of Ur." There he has three adventures, each with an appropriate heroic precedent. Craving to do a service for the Arnewi, he sets himself the task of ridding their cistern of the frogs that infest it and so threaten the land with famine. His American know-how back-fires, however, when not only the frogs are destroyed but the cistern as well, a result quite the opposite of that accomplished by another knight errant, Twain's Boss, who, in similar circumstances, restores the fountain in the Valley of Holiness in *A Connecticut Yankee in King Arthur's Court*. Henderson fares better in a wrestling match with Itelo, the English-speaking prince, who, like the beggar in the *Odyssey*, underestimates his man and finally succumbs to his superior, and clearly heroic, prowess. Just as Odysseus, Henderson must re-strain himself from utterly destroying his adversary: "But somehow I managed to keep a space clear in my brain for counsels of moderation." In a third test, like Gawain, Henderson withstands the romantic advances of Princess Mtalba, the sister of the queen of the Arnewi, who comes to entice him in his dwelling on the night before the exploit of the frogs.

More important than the three tests is Henderson's

encounter with the queen of the Arnewi, Queen Willatale, who reassures him that he has the will to live,
"Grun-tu-molani," in her language. Henderson rejoices:

> "Yes, yes, yes! Molani. Me molani. She sees that?
> God will reward her, tell her, for saying it to me.
> . . . Not only I molani for myself, but for everybody.
> I could not bear how sad things have become in the
> world and so I set out because of this molani."
> (P. 85)

The hero has received the secret word to sustain him,
and also a profound experience of life when the queen
greets him by placing his hand between her breasts.

> On top of everything else, I mean the radiant heat
> and the monumental weight which my hand received,
> there was the calm pulsation of her heart participating
> in the introduction. This was as regular as the rotation
> of the earth, and it was a surprise to me; my mouth
> came open and my eyes grew fixed as if I were touching
> the secrets of life. (P. 72)

Before he came to the land of the Arnewi, Henderson
had the desire to help others—this was his inheritance;
but the fiasco of the frogs proves knight errantry to be
not enough. Neither is the will to live, moving as his
encounter with Queen Willatale is. He must continue
his quest. When Romilayu, dejected by the turn of
events, suggests that they return to Baventai, the starting
place of their journey, Henderson replies that returning
to the States would mean death to him: "So if I quit
at this time I'll probably turn into a zombie. My face
will become as white as paraffin, and I'll lie upon my bed
until I croak."

Again the hero and his companion set out, traveling
across strange barren country for "nine or ten days"
until they reach the land of the Wariri, where they are

first met by a herdsman who looks like a Biblical figure, in particular "the man whom Joseph met when he went to look for his brothers, and who directed him along toward Dothan" where Joseph was thrown into the pit. In the land of the Wariri Henderson becomes a good friend of the King, Dahfu, and successfully passes two tests. He is strong enough to lift a great idol, the goddess Mummah, and for this he is made the tribal rainmaker and given the title Sungo. The second and more difficult task is facing a lion unafraid. For this crowning achievement Henderson must be carefully trained by King Dahfu on the many occasions when they descend into the pit where a captive lioness, Atti, is kept. "Transfer from lion to man is possible," Dahfu believes; Atti has much to teach and can make a change in Henderson if he acts like her. First, being "unavoidable," she will "force the present moment" upon Henderson. Second, she will teach him how to experience, for lions "are experiencers. But not in haste. They experience with deliberate luxury." The lesson of the importance of Beng is learned by becoming fully aware of the presence of the lion without fear: "When the fear yields, a beauty is disclosed in its place. This is also said of perfect love if I recollect, and it means that ego-emphasis is removed." Dahfu becomes a father surrogate like Dr. Tamkin, although he uses more primitive methods—a lion's den instead of a metropolitan commodity market —to bring his ward out of self-absorption. Dahfu inspires trust and love, even though he, too, is using the hero for ends that he doesn't announce—in this case the training of Henderson-Sungo for the kingship. With the conquest of fear and the recognition of Being, it will be possible to achieve the "high conduct" that Henderson could not seem to find in America. What Dahfu does not know is that the lion inspires in Henderson not only fear but a sense of guilt. Just before his departure from home he had attempted to kill a cat left behind by former tenants of one of his houses. At a distance of eight feet he aimed a pistol at the animal and missed, probably because his "will was not truly bent on his death." Even so, he confesses, "my heart was wrung by the memory, and I felt a tremendous sorrow. It had been a very close thing—almost a deadly sin." To complicate his guilty feeling, Lily, when she heard the shot, thought that he was trying to commit suicide as he had threatened many times. In his encounters with the lion Henderson remembers the cat and is troubled by "the obscure worry that my intended crime against the cat world might somehow be known here." Gradually, after many exposures, fear and guilt dissolve, and Henderson comes to the point when he is able to "act the lion" as his instructor requires. He has a sudden seizure, which, in its abandon and emotional depth, is something like Tommy Wilhelm's fit of weeping at the end of *Seize the Day.*

> And so I was the beast. I gave myself to it, and all my sorrow came out in the roaring. My lungs supplied the air but the note came from my soul. The roaring scalded my throat and hurt the corners of my mouth and presently I filled the den like a bass organ pipe. This was where my heart had sent me, with its clamor. Oh, Nebuchadnezzar! How well I understand that prophecy of Daniel. For I had claws, and hair, and some teeth, and I was bursting with hot noise. (P. 267)

Paradoxically, "being the beast" returns man to being human and in the end it is discovered that the human spirit determines all, that "the noble self-conception is everything. Put differently, you are in the flesh as your soul is." Thus "nature might be a mentality" and imagination can make us "rise to summits." In addition

to being, on the anthropological level, a piece of homeo-
pathic magic in which a man assumes the best qualities
of an animal, Henderson's experience with the lion is a
metaphysical exercise, a kind of religious revelation.
Dahfu is Henderson's hierophant, who brings his initiate
into contact with reality, with Being, as symbolized by
the lion. A man momentarily rebelling against civilization
is a fitting subject for these mysteries, as Ishmael facing
his whale, Ike McCaslin his bear (with the help of his
hierophant, Sam Fathers), and Santiago his marlin—all
of whom feel their humanity more keenly for the
experience.

Henderson's summit is not the transcendentalist's
contemplation but heroic action, and it is reached when
Henderson bravely attempts to rescue King Dahfu from
a lion that is "incompletely caught" in a lion trap. Much
like Francis Macomber in Hemingway's famous story,
Henderson proves that he has overcome his fear by
exposing himself to a lion at bay. Leslie Fiedler is
probably right in speculating that Eugene Henderson is
"a memoir and a tribute" to Ernest Hemingway.[9] We
note the similar physical appearance of the two men, the
flight from a tame, female-ridden America in pursuit of
heroic activity, the apprentice-hero's progress from fear
to courage under the tutelage of an accomplished master
of animals. It was the roaring of the lion that threw
Macomber into a state of fear the night before his
ignominious flight from the wounded lion; to Henderson
the snarling of the lion, in the final confrontation, is a
moment of truth that brings him face to face with
reality: "The snarling of this animal was indeed the
voice of death. . . . His voice was like a blow at the
back of my head." Just as Herzog had to save himself
from a false view of suffering, so Henderson must save
himself from a false view of reality, though there is no
dramatic blow with Herzog's discovery of the truth.

There are three in the career of Henderson: once while chopping wood he was struck by a flying log and got the idea "Truth comes with blows"; in wrestling with Itelo he received "a bad blow on the nose" and along with it the strange words, "I do remember well the hour that bursts the spirit's sleep." The third blow is the roaring of the lion, which brings to him at once the reality of death and the feeling of love. Henderson's sorrow over the fallen king, "the noblest guy I ever met," is true to form for epic heroes in its duration and soul-shaking depth, though it is expressed in jazzy terms:

> "Oh, King, King, I am a bad-luck type. I am a jinx, and death hangs around me. The world has sent you just the wrong fellow. I am contagious, like Typhoid Mary. Without me you would have been okay. You are the noblest guy I ever met. . . .
>
> Then I said, "Your Majesty, move over and I'll die beside you. Or else be me and live; I never knew what to do with life anyway, and I'll die instead." I began to rub and beat my face with my knuckles, crouching in the dust between the dead lion and the dying king. (P. 312)

Henderson's mourning continues even in Dahfu's tomb, where he and Romilayu are placed for safe-keeping against the time when Henderson-Sungo, the rainmaker, will become the new King. As Romilayu digs away at the wall separating them from the King's death chamber, Henderson, covered with dust, grieves. The death of his friend is "the hour that burst the spirit's sleep," and like Achilles he snaps out of his quarrel with life and recognizes for the first time the responsibility of greatness in men:

> "They say, Think big. Well, that's boloney of course, another business slogan. But greatness! That's another

thing altogether. Oh, greatness! Oh, God! Romilayu, I don't mean inflated, swollen, false greatness. I don't mean pride or throwing your weight around. But the universe itself being put into us, it calls out for scope. The eternal is bonded onto us. It calls out for its share. This is why guys can't bear to be so cheap. (P. 318)

Along with this larger, transcendental spirit Henderson is also moved by the ancient hero's desire for revenge: he wants to kill the Bunam, or priest, who tampered with the lion trap so that King Dahfu would fall into it and be destroyed.

After being kept three days in the tomb, Henderson is to be released by the tribesmen and crowned the new king of the Wariri. However, Henderson wants to return home, and with this in mind he and Romilayu plot their escape. Romilayu is to alarm their keepers with a cry that Sungo is dying and then place a stone in the hinge of the door as soon as it is opened by the guards; Henderson is then to fall upon the guards. The plan works and the two prisoners flee through the jungle in the direction of Baventai, the African village from which they had set out. Henderson insists upon taking with him the lion cub which had been left in the tomb with the body of the King; it was from this lion, the tribesmen believed, that the new king was to issue. To Henderson the cub represents the King, "a souvenir of a very dear friend . . . also an enigmatic form of that friend"; and it is Henderson's "bush-soul" a symbol of the new life and courage he has found in the jungle. Now he can return home a new man, one who has faced death, felt love, and discovered what true greatness is. The voice that had been driving him, he realizes at last, "wanted reality. How much unreality could it stand?" And the reality is heroism. The key experiences leading him to this self-realization are his encounters with Queen Willatale and King Dahfu. Quite unknown to him, they are the father and the mother he sought to bring back from death when he played the violin in his pig-farm days. Queen Willatale represents the principle of life, and Henderson's being struck with her is the hero's "winning of the bride" in Joseph Campbell's phrase. Henderson's association with Dahfu is the hero's "going to the father," an experience Campbell defines as a process that will "open his soul beyond terror to such a degree that he will be ripe to understand how the sickening and insane tragedies of this vast and ruthless cosmos are completely validated in the majesty of Being." [10] Being is the substance of Dahfu's instructions to Henderson in the lion cage.

The betrayal of Dahfu by the high priest, the three days that must elapse before a new king issues from the body of the dead king, the stone in the doorway (*lapis manalis*)—not rolled away but put there to keep the door open—echo the New Testament story of Christ's resurrection. Henderson is no Christ, however, but a hero returning to his home and family. After his escape he has but one thought: "I had to get back to Lily and the children, and especially Lily herself. I developed a bad case of homesickness." He is determined to make a new start in life, even begin the study of medicine. His mood is precisely like that of Herzog, who, at the end of his journey, reflects: "I mean to share with other human beings as far as possible and not destroy my remaining years in the same way." Out of deepest Africa and the primitive past Henderson travels in stages that repeat the course of civilization's march westward: the jungle, where he manages to survive by eating "cocoons and the larvae and ants"; Baventai, the Arab settlement on the edge of the jungle; Baktale, where his dysentery is controlled; Harar, in Ethiopia, where he parts from Romilayu and gives him his jeep, as he had promised; Khartoum and Cairo; Athens, where he feels compelled to see the Acropolis, but is disappointed; Rome and London, in which he has "no curiosity" even to see the sights; and Newfoundland. Although he is returning to civilization, he describes himself on his trip as "discontinuous with civilization." He is indeed like Odysseus cast upon the shore of Phaeacia. Practically naked in his flight from the Wariri, by the time he gets to Athens he is "still dressed as in Africa, same helmet, same rubber shoes"; in Rome he is still unshaved ("My beard had grown out considerably; on one side it gushed out half white but with many streaks of blond, red, black, and purple") and is now wearing "a corduroy outfit, burgundy colored, and an alpine hat with Bersagliere feathers." From the pre-historic past to the present, from savagery to civilization, from the tropics to the arctic, the triumphant hero travels home to life and the world of men.

Bellow does not treat us to the arrival of Henderson in New York, where he looks forward to being greeted by Lily. "Lily will have to sit up with me if it takes all night, I was thinking, while I tell her all about this." Instead there is a symbolic reunion of the wandering Odysseus with his wife and son. He makes friends with a stewardess who reminds him of Lily. Now that his quest is over and he is returning home, he allows himself to dwell on the feminine charms he had spurned in the person of Princess Mtalba. Of the stewardess he says:

Every twenty years or so the earth renews itself in young maidens. You know what I mean? Her cheeks had the perfect form that belongs to the young; her hair was kinky gold. Her teeth were white and posted on every approach. She was all sweet corn and milk. Blessings on her hips. Blessings on her thighs. (Pp. 333–34)

He cannot remember how many months he hasn't seen his wife. "You make me think of my wife," he says. The stewardess introduces him to a little boy who is traveling on the plane alone, an orphan, "a black-haired boy, like my own," thinks Henderson, and he spends the rest of the trip acting the father with him. During the stop-over at Newfoundland he is so overjoyed with the prospect of coming home to a new life that he wraps the boy in a blanket and runs around the plane:

> I told the kid, "Inhale. Your face is too white from your orphan's troubles. Breathe in this air, kid, and get a little color." I held him close to my chest. He didn't seem to be afraid that I would fall with him. While to me he was like medicine applied, and the air too; it was also a remedy. (P. 340)

The journey of Henderson is carefully planned by Bellow to represent stages between the poles of civilization and the primitive. From New York he flies, "an airborne seed," to Africa and is reborn on the scene of man's origin. Soon after arriving in Africa he parts company with the safari of his boyhood friend, Charlie Albert ("we were now, as then, in short pants") and hires a guide to take him even farther "out" in space and back in time. From the wrestling match with Itelo to the encounter with the lion at bay, Henderson must prove himself worthy of new life by undergoing a series of initiatory trials. Some of these are common to the grail quester: the blows he receives from man and beast, his polite rejection of Princess Mtalba's advances, the night he spends sitting up with a corpse. Other tests derive from anthropological sources, notably the exposure to the lion and the deathwatch over the body of Dahfu. Having fulfilled all requirements, the hero is ready for another rebirth, this time into civilization. However, it is not in New York but in Newfoundland that we finally leave him, "running—leaping, leaping, pounding, and tingling over the pure white lining of the gray Arctic silence," and there is no assurance that his new feeling will last once he gets home. Bellow leaves the issue open and will not claim for his volatile hero any more tangible achievement than he claims for his supine hero, Herzog, who similarly ends in silence: "At this time he had no messages for anyone. Nothing. Not a single word." Both have accomplished nothing beyond a possible change of spirit and a renewal of the desire to live, which is further than poor Tommy Wilhelm can go, though short of the emphatic resolution of personal affairs that distinguishes their ancient prototype.

To recapitulate the three odysseys before his latest novel: we have in each 1] a starting predicament in which a middle-aged man finds himself in despair because he is alienated from his family and unable to play a satisfying role in society, 2] a journey in which the hero exposes himself to peril, emotional if not physical, experiences strange encounters with death, and makes philosophical discoveries of great personal importance, and 3] an attempt to return to normal life through a reintegration with family and society and a clarification of the hero's identity.

Tommy Wilhelm is rejected by his father and spurned by his wife; he has never been able to make a successful career for himself either as an actor or businessman. Henderson is also rejected by his father, who never forgave him for being the survivor of three children; he cannot maintain normal relations with his wife and children, and in spite of being wealthy he cannot find anything to occupy himself with seriously for any length of time. Herzog's father and wife are enemies seeking to destroy him; he is no longer effective as a teacher and scholar, having abandoned both for jotting miniscule notes and writing letters he never mails. In each case, it is the personal dislocation of the individual, and not the sickness of society, that receives fullest attention.

Henderson's journey differs from the others in its strong primitive and dramatic accents; it is a return to the spirit of the Mexican adventures of Augie March. Herzog is a development and intellectual refinement of Tommy Wilhelm. In their sensitive immersion in metropolitan life, both characters seem to be truer expression of their author than Henderson, the compound of many prototypes, the wild man whose self-revelation comes through experiences with lions and dying kings in jungle places. Possibly Bellow himself parodies Henderson's sentimental regard for animals in his portrait of Herzog's friend Asphalter, who became the laughing-stock of Chicago when newspapers reported that he had tried to resuscitate his tubercular pet monkey by mouth-to-mouth respiration. Herzog is skeptical of the modern fashion for a man in trouble to "give himself, a failure, back to the species for a primitive cure."

While the tones and details vary in the three novels, their heroes share the idea that to find the meaning of life a man must discover the meaning of death, and their several journeys are devised to furnish them with experiences leading to the knowledge of death. Herzog is obsessed with the desire to communicate with the dead; many of his letters are written "to the dead, his own obscure dead, and finally the famous dead." In words echoing a familiar classical sentiment, he reaches out for the dead: "As the dead go their way, you want to call to them, but they depart in a black cloud of faces, souls." With his usual sense of moderation and capacity for self-correction, Herzog realizes that it is "a peculiar weakness of his character" to love the dead so well, to live with them "as much as with the living," and he must remind himself of the distinction between the fashionable "dread of death" and the hard-won realization "that life was life only when it was understood clearly as dying." Henderson is almost as equally concerned with death. In his bragging way he sees the encounter with death as another epic achievement for Americans, a task of the same order as "the Constitution and the Civil War and capitalism and winning the West." It is possible to read the whole of Henderson's journey as a journey into the land of the dead. The drought in the country of the Arnewi means death to men and cattle; King Dahfu is doomed to die and amuses himself juggling the skulls of his ancestors; indeed, from the time Henderson spends his first night among the Wariri in the same tent with a corpse (the former rain king) to his escape from Dahfu's tomb he is surrounded with death.

Tommy Wilhelm does not achieve reintegration with either family or society, but there is, as a result of his experiences, some clarification of his identity, which has been a source of serious trouble for him. When he went to Hollywood he changed his name from Wilhelm Adler to Tommy Wilhelm, hoping thereby to become a different sort of person. "He had never, however, succeeded in feeling like Tommy, and in his soul had always remained Wilky. . . . Wilky was his inescapable self." In the "underground corridor" scene and in the funeral-parlor scene, he does manage to overcome the horror of being Wilky by recognizing his kinship with humanity no matter how disfigured or pitiful. Henderson has a symbolical reunion with his family and presumably will devote himself to serving humanity as a doctor, while Herzog makes a partial return to family and home.

Tommy Wilhelm is Saul Bellow's tentative, perhaps unconscious, approach to the Odysseus motif, Henderson his full-blown serio-comic Odysseus, and Herzog his compromise. The unrelieved sadness of Tommy, his excessive self-pity, is corrected by the comic, outgoing

Henderson; the extravagances of Henderson are in turn corrected by Herzog, who returns to Tommy's world with just enough of Henderson's flair to offset a new intellectual burden. *In Seize the Day* Bellow brings the contemporary Odysseus to the shore and leaves him weaping there; in *Henderson the Rain King* he sends him on a traditionally patterned quest which ends just short of a triumphant return home; in *Herzog* he allows him to return to Ithaca and affords him a measure of success in keeping with the mood and limitations of contemporary life.

Mr. Sammler's Planet is Bellow's farewell to the theme of the contemporary Odysseus. In this version the perplexed hero is no longer the vigorous middle-aged man driven by the need to resolve his troubles, but an old man in his seventies who is at leisure to live "in kindly detachment, in farewell-detachment, in earth-departure objectivity." [11] His adventures are long since over—he was a Polish partisan in World War II—and now he is an observer and a listener of confessions. In the manner of the *Odyssey* and *Herzog*, Sammler's past travels are counterpointed with his present experiences, three days of encounters with family, friends, and strangers in New York City. These culminate in the death of his benefactor and nephew, Dr. Elya Gruner, and in a violent confrontation with a black pickpocket who has terrorized him on his frequent bus rides in the city. Impelled at last to act, Sammler is overcome by a horrible feeling:

> He was a man who had come back. He had rejoined life. He was near to others. But in some essential way he was also companionless. He was old. He lacked physical force. He knew what to do, but he had no power to execute it. . . . Sammler was powerless. To be so powerless was death. (P. 289)

Thus diminished, Sammler, a little while later, over the body of Dr. Gruner, can only offer, "in a mental whisper," a prayer of praise for his dead friend, in which the final words, in contrast to Henderson's "I want, I want, I want," are "we know, we know, we know" (p. 313). What each man knows is his duty as a man. Compromised even further than Herzog, Sammler is reduced to recognizing heroism in another man, Gruner, who was able, "even with a certain servility, to do what was required of him. . . . He was aware that he must meet, and he did meet—through all the confusion and degraded clowning of this life through which we are speeding—he did meet the terms of his contract" (p. 313).

6

Invisible Man

"All my life I have been looking for something," says the narrator of *Invisible Man*. That he remains nameless throughout the book is of the utmost importance, for the thing he is seeking is an identity he is doomed never to find. He is never called anything more precise than Boy and Brother. Consequently, the world cannot "see" him, cannot recognize individuality in him, although it still oppresses him as a member of a despised racial group and keeps him running from its wrath. He is a black Adam in a perverse Eden ruled by white men who are like gods: "the white folks, authority, the gods, fate, circumstances—the force that pulls your strings until you refuse to be pulled any more." In one striking passage the narrator reflects on the white men who furnished the scholarship money for him to attend a Negro college in the South as "those who had set me here in this Eden. . . . This was our world, they said as they described it to us, this our horizon and its earth, its seasons and its climate, its spring and its summer, and its fall and harvest some unknown millennium ahead; and these its floods and cyclones, and they themselves our thunder and lightning. . . ."[1] What specifically incurs the wrath of the gods against Boy is the offense he has given to Mr. Norton, one of the white trustees of the college. The college is partially Norton's creation; his "destiny is being made there" in the sense that his moral rectitude thrives on the assumption that his philanthropy is helping a deprived people. But Boy, in chauffering for Norton during one of his visits to the campus, inadvertently reveals to him some of the more horrible aspects of Negro life—an incestuous family and an orgiastic party of insane Negro war veterans— that flourish within a short distance of the well-kept campus. The roadhouse where the veterans regale themselves is called the Golden Day but resembles an inferno. Here Norton is confronted by a veteran named Burnside, who irreverently calls the relationship between Boy and Norton that of an automaton to his god and derides the idea that the college is Norton's destiny. Finally Boy rescues Norton from the "chaos" of the Golden Day, but he himself cannot escape the wrath. He is dismissed from college by President Bledsoe, a Negro who thrives by playing Uncle Tom to white philanthropists like Norton. Bledsoe furnishes Boy with letters of introduction devised to keep him looking for work in the land to which he is banished, the North. He is not aware that Bledsoe is determined never to readmit him to the college. With the departure of Boy from the campus, the myth of Eden comes to an end. Boy is the disobedient Adam who breaks one of the taboos of Eden (revealing how things really are there); Norton is the angry god, creator of the college; President Bledsoe in his archangel; Burnside is the Satan who questions the whole principle of Norton's relation to his creation and the creatures who inhabit it. Turned out of the Eden created for him by the white man in the South, the Negro sinner must now become a wanderer seeking a return home. The story of Odysseus takes over from the story of Eden.

Covering a period of twenty years, the narrator's adventures, like those of Odysseus, are of two distinct kinds, real and fabulous. The period in the South, from early youth to his dismissal from college, is done in a more or less realistic manner, while the series of adventures following, in New York, are clearly of the fantastic sort and are done in a surrealistic style. Ellison himself distinguishes three styles in the book: the "naturalistic treatment" of the Southern experiences, the expressionistic treatment of Boy's transition from South to North, and the surrealistic style in which the disillusionment of Boy in the North is done.[2] However, there does not seem to be much justification for making a distinction between the styles of the last two sections of the book.

Surrealistic or realistic, the experiences of the hero are cast in a single pattern repeated over and over again: he tries out a certain identity as a Negro in America, meets with disaster in this role, and drops it to begin over again with a new identity. This cycle is expressed by Ellison in the metaphors of death and rebirth. Each time the hero fails in a certain role he figuratively dies; his hopeful assumption of a new role is signified by the imagery of rebirth. There are two major "deaths"—one following the end of his experience as a southern Negro and one following his experience as a Negro in the North at the end of the book, and two major rebirths—one initiating the hero into life in the North and one at the start of his last role as a member of an organization called the Brotherhood. In addition there are many minor deaths and rebirths, and altogether they constitute a kind of repetitive rhythm. This proves to be too monotonous for some readers, but seen against the background of the Negro novel in America the rebirth archetype is a natural enough, even inevitable, device serving two important purposes: it takes a Negro character in a condition of material and psychological deprivation and suddenly endows him with the capacity for sensitive reactions necessary for the central figure of a novel, and it expresses the hope of the American Negro for a new identity and a new kind of life. The rebirth archetype is a perfect reflection of the Negro author's desire for literary expressiveness and the Negro people's yearning for freedom. Richard Wright and James Baldwin share with Ellison a keen interest in rebirth imagery.[3] The morning after murdering and dismembering a white woman Bigger Thomas in *Native Son* rises from sleep a new man: "He had murdered and had created a new life for himself." Damon Cross in *The Outsider* takes a new identity after he is presumed dead in a subway train accident, which Wright turns into an elaborate death and rebirth image. As in the case of Bigger, the black man's new life is made possible only at the cost of the death of whites: in order to extricate himself from the wreckage Cross must hammer away at the face of a white man and step on the corpse of a white woman. In part three of James Baldwin's *Go Tell It on the Mountain*, appropriately entitled "The Threshing Floor," fourteen-year-old John Grimes sinks to the "dusty place" in front of the altar of a storefront church in Harlem and experiences sensations of dying and being reborn. Johnny's rebirth is a thoroughly Christian initiation into the life of suffering of the American Negro; Bigger, Cross, and Ellison's Boy are reborn into an illusory equality with whites.

Ellison may have found in *Huckleberry Finn* precedent for the use of the death-rebirth cycle as a method of structuring a novel.[4] From the time that he plants evidence of his "murder" to the last episode at the Phelps farm, Huck undergoes a series of escapes from one kind of life and immersions into another, with the river acting as a kind of limbo between lives. The imagery of death and rebirth occasionally marks these transitions. In his last incarnation Huck is reborn as Tom Sawyer, and when the Phelps family express their delight in seeing

"Tom," Huck reflects: "But if they was joyful, it warn't nothing to what I was; for it was like being born again, I was so glad to find out who I was." Huck doesn't mind being Tom because he is so firmly in possession of his true identity, but loss of identity is no joke for Boy (any more than the flight to freedom is for Jim), and Boy does not have the river to fall back on between sorties into the world.

Rebirth imagery is first used in *Invisible Man*, not in relation to the hero, but in the story of the man who founded the college which the hero attends. Every spring, the student body, officials, and white trustees gather in the chapel on Founder's Day to honor the memory of the man who rose from slavery to the leadership of his people. The life story of the Founder is movingly told by Rev. Homer A. Barbee, a blind minister, and it incorporates elements of the life and resurrection of Christ with details of the death and burial of Lincoln as celebrated in Whitman's "When Lilacs Last in the Dooryard Bloom'd." The Founder was born to a slave woman and survived an attack from an insane cousin: "he lay nine days in a deathlike coma and then suddenly and miraculously recovered. You might say that it was as though he had risen from the dead or been reborn." He became "a humble prophet," a "black Aristotle," carrying the message of freedom to multitudes of Negroes and doing his best to patch up the rift between whites and Negroes in the nation. He died from "a sudden and mysterious sickness" while traveling on a train. His end was presaged by the disappearance from the sky of "the looming great North Star." The train then became "a veritable train of sorrow visited by people who "came to pay their respects at the stations" amid the "weeping bugles" and "funeral crape." At the interment "a single wild rose tossed farewell." But the Founder's death is not to be thought of as the end, continues Reverend Barbee. "A great seed had been planted. A seed which has continued to put forth its fruit in its season as surely as if the great creator had been resurrected." The college has grown to be a great institution and Dr. Bledsoe, its President, has become the Founder's "living agent, his physical presence."

The story of the Founder is loosely modeled after the lifework of Booker T. Washington, in particular his establishment of Tuskegee Institute and his effort to bring about a reconciliation between whites and blacks in the period following Reconstruction. Boy's ambition is to be like Washington, whose great Atlanta Exposition speech he quotes in his own high-school graduation address. Consequently, Founder's Day celebration has all the more striking effect upon Boy, who, being in disgrace with the President for having acted indiscreetly in the presence of a white trustee, fears that he will never distinguish himself like the Founder. His misconduct is a betrayal of the Founder's dream; for him there can be no freedom, no glorious death and resurrection. Of course the narrator does not know at this time that the College and President Bledsoe are false and depend upon a despicable subservience to white men, that Founder's Day is simply an occasion for the white trustees to celebrate their own virtues as friends of the under-privileged: "not merely acting out the myth of their goodness, and wealth and success and power and benevolence and authority in cardboard masks, but themselves, these virtues concretely!" This ironical view the narrator cannot have until his point of view becomes retrospective later on in his life, and so his dismissal from college seems a kind of death to him, "like the parting of flesh."

The first major death-and-rebirth of the narrator does not occur until a little later in New York where he has gone to seek work, armed with the worthless letters of introduction. In a paint factory, where he finally finds a job, he is involved in an accident, an explosion in which he is "shot forward with sudden acceleration into a wet blast of black emptiness that was somehow a bath of whiteness." Then there is the familiar association of death with falling and a period in which he lies "transfixed and numb with the sense that I had lost irrevocably an important victory." The hospital treatment following the accident is an elaborate rebirth conceit in which the narrator is like an infant being born and the medical equipment a womb. Unable to identify himself to the nurse and two doctors, he thinks of ways to destroy the machine in which he is lying, but since he cannot do that without destroying himself he gives up the idea. Then he is "delivered."

> I saw their hands at the lid, loosening the bolts, and before I could react they had opened the lid and pulled me erect. . . .
> I felt a tug at my belly and looked down to see one of the physicians pull the cord which was attached to the stomach node, jerking me forward. . . .
> I recoiled inwardly as though the cord were part of me. Then they had it free and the nurse clipped through the belly band and removed the heavy node. I opened my mouth to speak but one of the physicians shook his head. They worked swiftly. The nodes off, the nurse went over me with rubbing alcohol. (P. 185)

One of the attendants remarks, "You're a new man," and indeed the narrator thereafter discovers new abilities and potentialities in himself—the ability for example, to use words and express attitudes that he does not recognize as his own. Most important, he is "no longer afraid. Not of the important men, not of the trustees and such; for knowing now that there was nothing which I could expect from them, there was no reason to be afraid." The narrator as an innocent southern boy has died, and he is reborn in the North as an intelligent, sensitive freedom-fighter. Such is the transformation of Bigger Thomas in *Native Son* from an "overgrown adolescent" to "a cunning and introspective fugitive" and the transformation of Damon Cross from postal employee to Communist conspirator.

A mark of Boy's new sophistication is the ironic tone running through his entire experience of rebirth. The ideas of procreation and motherhood are ridiculed by association with childhood rhymes which were once innocent amusements and now suggest obscene meanings as they pass through his drugged mind:

> *Buckeye the Rabbit*
> *Shake it, shake it*
> *Buckeye the Rabbit*
> *Break it, break it. . . .*
> (P. 184)

He is asked by the attendant who Brer Rabbit was. "He was your mother's back-door man, I thought. Anyone knew they were one and the same: 'Buckeye' when you were very young and hid yourself behind wide innocent eyes; 'Brer,' when you were older." A song his grandmother sang now appears as a travesty of the traditional story of the creation of life on earth:

> *Godamighty made a monkey*
> *Godamighty made a whale*
> *And Godamighty made a 'gator*
> *With hickeys all over his tail. . . .*
> (P. 178)

A song he knew as a child comes to mind:

> *Did you ever see Miss Margaret boil water?*
> *Man, she hisses a wonderful stream,*

Seventeen miles and a quarter,
Man, and you can't see her pot for the steam. . . .[5]

(P. 179)

"But now the music became a distinct wail of female pain." The innocence of childhood has concealed latent obscenity, and the whole experience of rebirth marks the transition of the narrator not only from the South to the North but from the ignorance of youth to the bitter knowledge of adulthood.

The ironical mood does not persist, however. After he leaves the hospital to begin life again in Harlem, our hero witnesses the scene with "wild infant's eyes" and is taken in and nursed back to health by a kindly woman named Mary Rambo. From her he learns the gospel of service to others, especially to his race, which he is encouraged to lead "on up a little higher." Mary becomes a true mother to him, not the machine mother of his hospital hallucinations, "a force, a stable, familiar force like something out of my past which kept me from whirling off into some unknown which I dared not face." But, like the knight Percival, he must at last leave his second mother in order to become a member of the Brotherhood, an organization eager to make use of the rabble-rousing ability he accidentally displayed at an eviction proceeding in Harlem. "What a vast difference between Mary and those for whom I was leaving her," he reflects. "And why should it be this way, that the very job which might make it possible for me to do some of the things which she expected of me required that I leave her?" Later, when he is in flight from the Brotherhood, he attempts unsuccessfully to go back to Mary.

His initiation into the Brotherhood is accomplished in a scene that is curiously fashioned to resemble the classical descent of the Odyssean hero into the underworld in order to learn about his role in the future. To get to the place where the Brotherhood is meeting he is driven across Manhattan in an automobile, "through Central Park, now completely transformed by the snow," close by the "zoo with its dangerous animals" and "the reservoir of dark water, all covered by snow and by night, by snow-fall and by night-fall, buried beneath black and white, gray mist and gray silence." On the marquee of the building he enters is the word Chthonian; a "bronze door-knocker in the shape of a large-eyed owl" produces "an icy peal of clear chimes." He moves "past the uniformed doorman with an un-canny sense of familiarity." The strangeness of the whole experience is augmented by the narrator's "sense that I had somehow been through it all before. I couldn't decide if it were from watching some similar scene in the movies, from books I'd read, or from some recurrent but deeply buried dream." From Brother Jack, the leader of the Brotherhood, the hero learns about his future: he is to be "the true interpreter of the people . . . the new Booker T. Washington." In times of crisis, Brother Jack assures him, "the people look back to the dead to give them a clue." The new member of the Brotherhood is properly impressed: "I had the sense of being present at the creation of important events, as though a curtain had been parted and I was being allowed to glimpse how the country operated." Even more important, he sees his membership in the Brotherhood as an opportunity to fulfill his boyhood ambition to become another Booker T. Washington. He is assured by Jack that "Booker Washington was resurrected today at a certain eviction in Harlem."

Another rebirth ritual is required to mark the be-ginning of Brother's life as a political agitator, and this occurs appropriately when he is presented to a mass protest meeting organized by the Brotherhood. After approaching the meeting hall by going "up the alley through the tunneling dark," he enters the great arena where the audience is singing "John Brown's body lies a-mould'ring in the grave" and is introduced. The floodlights in which he stands create "a semi-transparent curtain" between him and the audience: "I felt the hard, mechanical isolation of the hospital machine and I didn't like it." Brother quickly recovers and delivers a very moving speech. "Something strange and miraculous and transforming is taking place in me right now," he tells the crowd. But this time it is his entry into humanity, not simply life, that is noted; he has "come home" to his "true family" and people: "I feel that here tonight, in this old arena, the new is being born and the vital old revived. In each of you, in me, in us all." No irony touches this experience, which seems to place Brother in the glorious tradition of the Founder, but there is one ominous note. Just before he enters the hall, Brother is met by an old man who lives in "a Hooverville shanty" between "a great abandoned hole that had been the site of a sports arena" and a railroad yard. "Stooped and dark and sprouting rags from his shoes, hat and sleeves, he shuffled slowly toward me, bringing a threatening cloud of carbolic acid." Like a prophet foreboding nothing good, the old man, a syphilitic, stands at the edge of Brother's new life,—just as Steinbeck's Hooverville prophet warns the Joads before they arrive in California. Brother pauses only for a moment, for his success at the meeting seems to open a new career for him.

Brother's rebirth coincides with his return home. As in the case of Odysseus, he who had been thought dead lives again and he lives in order to lead his people out of their troubles. Boy has returned home, not to the South which he had formerly thought was home but to his people wherever they may be. The task found at home by this latter-day Odysseus is curiously the same as his prototype's: he must seek to end the dispossession of his people. The dispossession of the Negro in America is actually the subject of his speech, the climactic line of which is "We'll be dispossessed no more!" Even before joining the Brotherhood, Boy had called attention to himself by arousing a street crowd against an eviction proceeding in Harlem, and as he takes his place on the platform in the arena the audience chants, "No more dispossessing of the dispossessed." His speech in the arena is but the continuation of his fight against dispossession.

The fable up to this point bears a resemblance to the *Odyssey*: A man is cast out into the world because of the wrath of the gods; he becomes a wanderer seeking a return to his home and exchanging one identity for another as he makes his perilous way through the world. He descends into the underworld and learns his fate; returns to his homeland and consecrates himself to the task of putting an end to the dispossession of his people. But this Odysseus is not strong enough, nor resourceful enough, to cleanse the kingdom and turn out the spoilers; he must work through the Brotherhood, an organization which he finally learns is no more interested in the rescue of the Negro than the College had been. Again he finds that the white man is using the Negro and his plight for his own moral aggrandizement and that any Negro who helps him is his dupe. The leftist leader of the Brotherhood, Jack, is as much "the great white father" as Norton, the capitalist. The world, specifically the world of the white man, is a monstrous Cyclops and the narrator is an invisible Odysseus. In the one instance in which the relationship of the Greek myth to the present narrative is made explicit, Brother Jack is berating Brother for his having initiated an action on behalf of Negroes without consulting the central committee. Suddenly, because of his anger, Jack's left eye, an artificial one, pops out of its socket into a glass of water: "He stopped, squinting at me with Cyclopean irritation. . . . He slammed the glass upon the table, splashing the water on the back of my hand. I shook like a leaf. . . . He doesn't even see me" (p. 359).

Brother's association with the Brotherhood and his life in the North are brought to a close in a series of scenes similar in their phantasmagoric quality to those which ended his career in the South. The scenes in which Boy and Norton visit the Trueblood family and the Golden Dawn typify the chaotic condition of Negro life in the rural South, while the Harlem scenes at the end of the book just as surely typify the breakdown of Negro life in the urban North. They are based on the Harlem riot of 1943 and present a picture of unruly mobs looting stores, burning buildings, defying the police, and finally turning upon each other.

On the day before the Harlem riot Brother delivers the funeral oration at the burial of Tod Clifton, a dear friend who had been killed by a policeman in a senseless street incident. Brother blames himself for Clifton's death ("my anger helped speed his death") and, without conferring with the Brotherhood, plans the funeral demonstration as "a means of avenging him and preventing other such deaths." Now in fear of being severely disciplined, he meets a Brotherhood leader's wife from whom he hopes to learn what is in store for him. Her name is Sybil and she frequents the bar at the Chthonian. On the night of the riot, "a hot dry August night," she drags Brother in the direction of Harlem:

> We tottered before an ancient-looking building, its windows dark. Huge Greek medallions showed in spots of light upon its facade, above a dark labyrinthine pattern in the stone, and I propped her

against the stoop with its carved stone monster. She leaned there, her hair wild, looking at me in the street light, smiling. Her face kept swinging to one side, her right eye desperately closed. (Pp. 399–400)

He finally succeeds in ditching the drunken woman and proceeds by himself to Harlem, which by this time is a raging inferno.

In the selection Ellison makes of the details of Brother's journey from midtown Manhattan to Harlem, we have another transformation of familiar New York places into the landscape of the mythical underworld. Having buried his fallen comrade and consulted Sybil, Brother continues on his way, clutching his golden bough, a briefcase containing all of his lifetime identification papers. He takes a bus going north on Riverside Drive, the Hudson River on his left, "the swiftly unfolding blur of anchored boats, dark water and lights pouring past. . . . I was as if drowned in the river." He passes Grant's Tomb, "crowned with a red light of warning," and George Washington Bridge, "the monumental bridge, ropes of light across the dark river." On the other side of the river he can discern the cliffs of the Palisades, "their revolutionary agony lost in the riotous lights of roller coasters." Alighting from the bus on the Riverside embankment, he descends to 125th Street, which marks the boundary of Harlem. At the cost of straining a metaphor, Ellison imagines the street as a river "with waves of cobblestones." Undeterred, Brother crosses "the hard stone river of the street" and enters Harlem proper. Still one more obstacle must be passed, a flight of birds which resemble the Harpies of Virgil in their filth, hint of prophecy, and location just outside of the inferno of Harlem. They foul the air and streak his jacket with an "encrusted barrage"; their "myriad-voiced humming" seems to carry a message for him: "it was as though they had been waiting for me and no one but me—dedicated and set aside for me—for an eternity."

Among other wild adventures in Harlem that night, Brother plays a heroic part in a battle with a man named Ras, a black nationalist and leader of an organization resembling the Black Muslims. Ras of course sees the riot as an ideal opportunity to inaugurate his war against white man, and he leads his group like an army. He is mounted on "a great black horse" and is "dressed in the costume of an Abyssinian chieftain; a fur cap upon his head, his arm bearing a shield, a cape made of the skin of some wild animal around his shoulders." A bitter opponent of the Brotherhood because of its white leadership, Ras hurls a spear at Brother when he recognizes him and orders his followers to hang him. The spear misses and Brother hurls it back at Ras, feeling a surge of heroic fervor and renewed life. Appropriately, the spear rips through both cheeks, locking the jaws of Ras the Exhorter. Heroism is short-lived, however, as Brother recognizes that he and Ras have reached the uttermost absurdity, Negroes fighting among themselves over differing interpretations of a reality controlled by white man. It is better, he concludes, "to live out one's own absurdity than to die for that of others, whether Ras's or Jack's," and he flees before the followers of Ras ("They came behind me like a draft of flames. . . .") and, a little later, before a gang of bat-wielding whites.

The narrator's last identity, a Negro working for his people within a white organization, thus comes to naught, and he experiences again a figurative death, this time falling into a manhole in the street, a deeper part of hell, where he lies "in the black dark upon the black coal." He later falls asleep: "I moved off over the black water, floating, sighing . . . sleeping invisibly." In order to see in the hole the next morning, Brother has to burn the papers in his briefcase, and these happen to be the papers signifying the various roles he has played in his travels—his high school diploma, one of President Bledsoe's letters of recommendation, the slip on which Jack had written the name assigned to him by the Brotherhood. Here is the familiar recapitulation of the epic hero's career, but without pride or issue.

The "underground" is literally a "basement that was shut off and forgotten during the nineteenth century." Ironically, this underground is not in shadow but is illuminated by 1,369 electric light bulbs, and the man who has been invisible in the world aboveground is now a form rather than a shade or ghost. "Without light I am not only invisible," he reflects, "but formless as well; and to be unaware of one's form is to live a death. I myself, after existing some twenty years, did not become alive until I discovered my invisibility." [6] Brother's underworld has the traditional depths within depths. Under the influence of marijuana he discovers a new way of listening to music, "hearing not only in time, but in space as well. I not only entered the music but descended, like Dante, into its depths." Music becomes an underworld wherein he finds "a beautiful girl the color of ivory pleading in a voice like my mother's" and, on an even lower level, a preacher addressing a colored congregation on the text the "Blackness of Blackness."

There seems to be no possibility of recovery from this death and nothing to learn from "this underworld of sound" in which he hears an "old singer of spirituals" tell him, "Go curse your God, boy, and die." No further rebirth seems possible as he dreams of being castrated by his enemies, and there is no use in seeking other identities since no identity has helped him in the way Odysseus was helped by his several disguises. In spite of his many efforts, for this wanderer there is no return home as there presumably is for Henderson, and his descent into the underworld brings him nothing but a deeper despair for his people and his own failure to help them. The odysseys of the Founder and, by implication, Booker T. Washington, may have ended in false accomplishments, but Brother's ends in none whatsoever. The answer to the question Brother had asked when he set out on his travels—"How could I ever return home?" —is given at the end of his journey: "No, I couldn't return to Mary's, or to the campus, or to the Brotherhood, or home." A burial alive seems to be the fate of Brother, a grave remaining a grave, not a coffin becoming a lifebuoy.

Yet Ellison refuses to write an utterly hopeless ending to his hero's adventures. At the very last, Brother begins to regard his stay in the underground not as death but a hibernation that can have an end; the "stench in the air . . . might be the smell either of death or of spring —I hope of spring." Perhaps his adventures have not been for nothing, for even though he has not found an identity or made good his return home, "there's a possibility that even an invisible man has a socially responsible role to play." And that role is to tell white men how they have failed to see the Negro in America as a human being, to tell them "what was really happening when your eyes were looking through." This idea is raised to a universal level with the suggestion, at the very end of the book, that perhaps the black man's predicament is Everyman's predicament, that all men are as invisible to one another as the Negro is to the white man, that his experience is simply a dramatic symbol of theirs. The narrator closes his account with the ominous words. "Who knows but that, on the lower frequencies, I speak for you?"

To some readers this hopeful note in the Epilogue is an unearned piece of optimism in view of the failure of every one of Brother's previous excursions. No hero can exist in this "death-driven novel," writes Marcus

Klein,[7] and Brother admits as much himself when he reflects that he is "no hero, but short and dark with only a certain eloquence and a bottomless capacity for being a fool to mark me from the rest." Nothing can be expected from his emergence from hiding but a recurrence of his past failures. Robert Bone defines the "basic image" of the novel as a "withdrawal from humanity into an underground den." [8] There is to be remembered, however, the cycle of death and rebirth, the rhythm of commitment and withdrawal, which is as strong in *Invisible Man* as it is in *Huckleberry Finn.* The Odyssean drive to return home alternates with the modern hero's withdrawal. Tension in Ellison's novel is created by placing the contemporary theme of "the modern self in recoil," as defined by Ihab Hassan,[9] against the background of traditional heroic patterns that prove to be ineffectual. Instead of working for the hero, the old mainstays fall away: his Sybil is a drunken nymphomaniac who is interested in nothing more than being "raped" by a Negro; his mentor, Jack, is an organization tyrant who conceives of heroism as a "blind" sacrifice to party discipline; there is no dependable brotherhood of warriors, no clear cause to fight for. Brother's quest is thus unsuccessful; his story falls into Frye's category of the "ironic or satiric epic . . . in which every quest, however successful and heroic, has sooner or later to be made over again." [10]

But Brother is not only representative of the contemporary hero as "self-deprecating *eiron*" (in Hassan's definition); he takes his place alongside of two American heroes of the past who are noted for their withdrawal from heroic action, Ishmael and Huck Finn. Together with Brother they make an interesting development of the depreciation of heroism. Although Ishmael remains aloof from the chase, in witnessing the exploits of Ahab he gives us a splendid, sympathetic portrait of the grand epic hero. Huck Finn, very much like Brother, withdraws from society after sampling various kinds of heroic commitment and finding himself a bungler and others false. Through his ironical acceptance of the extravagances of Tom Sawyer, Huck gives us a parody of the traditional "book" hero. Yet, almost by accident, Huck does succeed in achieving something rare, something which Brother considers a desperate necessity: a white, Huck is able to bring himself to see a Negro. Brother achieves nothing, unless it can be argued, by going outside of the book and into history, that he too performed a chance feat by having played a part in the Harlem riot of 1943, which, as a precursor of the riots of 1967, may be said to have helped make the Negro visible in America!

The ending of *Invisible Man* is indeterminate. The cycle of death and rebirth is bound to continue, although there is certainly not in this work "the merely irresponsible irony of a turning cycle" which Frye finds in *Finnegans Wake*. There is "hope of spring," but Brother's only use now seems to be in representing the despairing thought that the humanity of all men, black or white, is never perceived and acted upon and that no man can find a satisfactory role to play in life. Even if there is a new life for him, Brother will emerge from underground alone and unsung, his identity not the returning hero's but simply Everyman's. Further participation in communal action will avail nothing, for he has exhausted the possibilities in his previous lives. Among whites, the political left, the Brotherhood, offers no more help to the Negro than the political right, represented by Southern businessmen and Northern philanthropists. Among Negroes, black nationalists, represented by Ras and his cohorts, are found to be as foolhardy and ineffectual as the traditional Uncle Toms, like the Founder and President Bledsoe. There seem to be no more journeys to make; and Brother's ending is no beginning, as it is for his more fortunate white contemporary, Henderson. Brother's travels end in the glare of 1,369 electric lights in a forgotten basement, not in the invigorating air of the New World. His is a black odyssey in more ways than one.

7

The Continuing Tradition

The epic tradition in the twentieth-century American novel begins with Frank Norris's many-faceted examination in *The Octopus* of the possibilities of heroic action in an economic situation; these he finally rejects in favor of a cosmic law governing men and making their conflicts vain. Moved by the needs of their time, Steinbeck and Hemingway restore the epic hero and the communal sacrifice for a cause, no matter how desperate and how sordid the circumstances may be. *The Octopus* ends with the scattering of the forces of the ranchers, the dispersal of a *comitatus*, whereas *The Grapes of Wrath* and *For Whom the Bell Tolls* present the simple beginnings of communities committed to purposeful action. Homer, declares Kenneth Rexroth, "portrays heroic valor as fundamentally destructive, not just of social order but of humane community." [1] Such is the viewpoint of Norris and to some extent of Ellison as well. Steinbeck and Hemingway reflect rather the tradition of the *Aeneid* when they show how violence brings divided people together into a *comitatus*, though theirs is a *comitatus* of commoners, from whose midst issues a hero. "Alone a man is nothing" are the dying words of Richard Wright's hero in *The Outsider*; in 1953 this sentiment came at the end of a long series of similar declarations. In joining Communist labor organizers Jim Nolan in Steinbeck's *In Dubious Battle* is careful not to repeat the error of his father, "who always had to fight alone. He got licked every time." In his dying moments Hemingway's Hank Morgan, the hero of *To Have and Have Not*, comes to the same conclusion: "One man alone ain't got. No man alone now." The necessity of concerted action, discovered in the two earlier books of Steinbeck and Hemingway, comes to flower in *The Grapes of Wrath* and *For Whom the Bell Tolls*, whose didacticism is devoted to driving that point home again and again. "You felt an absolute brotherhood with the others," Robert Jordan confesses to himself, and Tom Joad concurs with the feeling that "a soul wasn't no good 'less it was with the rest." Both young men surrender their identities and their lives to dedicate themselves to a band of fighters, Jordan to the Spanish Loyalists and Tom to the leaders of the new proletariat.

An extreme, late statement of the brotherhood of fighters occurs in James Jones's *From Here to Eternity* (1951). Although it comes after World War II, this novel, like *For Whom the Bell Tolls*, is devoted to the preparation of the spirit of man for the rigors of war. It moves the American soldier closer to World War II than Hemingway's book by bringing him up to the baptism of fire at Pearl Harbor. In spite of its sordid picture of human behavior in the large, it supports an image of incorrigible heroism in the characterization of Robert E. Lee Prewitt. Ironically, it is the rebellious man, the deserter, the criminal who turns out to be the likeliest candidate for wartime heroics, and it is a group of prisoners in an Army stockade who make the best training ground for heroism, the true brotherhood of fighters. Of all the men in his company Prewitt alone remains uncorrupted by a peacetime military organization and holds onto a strict sense of honor, which he has inherited from "the old hungry tradition" of

American "woodsmen and the ground-clearing farmers."
Like Ahab, whom Melville describes as "a man cut
away from the stake, when the fire has overruningly
wasted all the limbs without consuming them, or taking
away one particle from their compacted aged robust-
ness," [2] so Prewitt has been "sifted and resifted and then
sifted again, until all the dry rot had been winnowed out,
all the soft spots squeezed out, all the rotting gangrene
. . . excised out, so that only the firm hardy remainder
of the most absolute of toughness, that would not only
hold its own but would triumph, in a whole world of
toughness, was all that was left now." [3] A fellow stockade
prisoner, Jack Malloy, is Prewitt's mentor, a leftist saint
and prophet of a new socialist religion. Malloy and
Prewitt are in the same tradition as Caraher and Presley,
Casy and Tom Joad, General Golz and Robert Jordan,
Brother Jack and Brother. After the Japanese attack
Pearl Harbor, Prewitt, who has been AWOL, risks his
life to return to his company and earns the epitaph of
the American guards who mistakenly shoot him down,
"So he is a soljer, after all." His self-sacrifice is futile,
but his example lives on in Sergeant Warden, the professional soldier whose whole Army career has been
devoted to staying on top of the peacetime situation in
his company. Warden is deeply impressed by Prewitt's
heroism, which he dares not name ("you were no
Carolingian douzeper, you were no Robert of Locksley")
but nonetheless recognizes when he admits that
"Prewitt seemed to hold the key to something," that
"Prewitt had become a symbol to him of something."

Grieving over the transformation of human life that
has collapsed "the long-inherited, timeless universe of
symbols," Joseph Campbell closes his study of the hero
with the despondent view that "there is no society any
more as the gods once supported. . . . Isolated societies,
dream-bounded with a mythologically charged horizon,

no longer exist except as areas to be exploited." [4] Julian Hartt concurs when he writes, "Perhaps for Melville, and for Conrad too, the community which alone creates the epic and can be instructed by it has vanished." [5] To this view of the inauspiciousness of the times it must be objected that gods die unaccountably in all times, or the conditions in which they prosper change in both primitive and advanced societies; it is precisely then that poets redouble their efforts to keep them alive. The writer of epic, whether he be Homer or Melville, is always imagining "isolated societies" or communities reflecting considerably more mythic significance than their creators' times actually allow. Such societies are the crew of the *Pequod*, Hemingway's partisans, Steinbeck's Okies and paisanos, Bellow's Africans, and Jones's stockade prisoners. In drawing upon the epic tradition, the writers we have considered cover the raw facts of contemporary economic and political warfare with an aura of mythic sanctity that is productive of heroes and heroic action.

The overstatement of heroic valor in Steinbeck, Hemingway, and their followers made reaction inevitable after World War II when the antiwar sentiment bred from World War I was resumed by a new generation of writers. Norman Mailer is the most representative of these and his *The Naked and the Dead* the most ambitious attempt to present the whole picture of modern military action from the overall strategy of commanding generals to the minutest details of individual survival. The story is thus given epic proportions, and Mailer gets it told by alternating innumerable narrative blocks of present action with flashbacks of the life-histories of ten individuals. A "Chorus" consisting of the collective monologues of enlisted men adds a third component to an episodic structure very similar to the montage organization of Dos Passos's *U.S.A.* Even though a specific military mission lends a direction to the massive accumulation of detail that is not to be found in the earlier novel, the final result is the same in both books: the degradation of character and human enterprise. War, rather than commercial civilization, is the environment, but futility waits equally upon the efforts of man to transcend his environment. The reconnaissance patrol, whose mission is to reconnoiter behind enemy lines in Mailer's synecdoche of the war in the Pacific, has the same opportunity as the partisans in *For Whom the Bell Tolls*; as its ranking sergeant states the case, "if we could make this patrol okay, it might tie up the campaign." And there is a transcendent as well as military objective, scaling Mount Anaka, the imposing peak that lies between the American and Japanese positions on the island. The mountain is the only thing that inspires awe in the men. With Sergeant Croft the assault on the mountain amounts to a monomania on the scale of Ahab's: "Again, he felt a crude ecstasy. He could not have given the reason, but the mountain tormented him, beckoned him, held an answer to something he wanted. It was so pure, so austere." [6] The patrol's mission and climbing the mountain end farcically: Croft himself accidentally slams into a hornets' nest, and the men, maddened by stings and completely beyond Croft's control, run pell-mell down the mountainside. Their journey along the jungle floor to reach the mountain slope was like a journey through hell; their painful ascent was like an ascent of Mount Purgatory; but they never reach the peak, the promised paradise.

In Mailer's anti-epic the oppressive burden of naturalistic detail remains unrelieved by the sort of transcendent compensation found in the rescue of Maria and the survival of the Joads. There is no band of devoted men; the reconnaissance patrol never functions as a fighting unit, each man being an isolated, distrustful enemy of his neighbor. From such a group no hero can emerge, although there are three possible candidates for heroic honors in the book. Of these the likeliest is Lieutenant Hearn, who has the same opportunity as Robert Jordan: leading a small unit in a mountain pass. But Hearn lacks Jordan's prowess and has no predecessor, nor loyal companion, nor proper mentor; and his liberalism is not nearly as confident. To his dismay he discovers that the motives impelling him to action are those of the two most corrupt characters among his acquaintance: General Cummings, a supreme egotist whose sole delight is the exercise of power over masses of people, and Sergeant Croft, who is driven by a lust to hate and kill. The weak liberal is thus assuming Fascist virtues! It is a mercy, perhaps, that he does not survive; the general assigns Hearn to the patrol and the sergeant sees to it that he is killed by the enemy. But crushing poor Hearn is all that these forceful men have to show for their ruthlessness, for, in spite of his acute understanding of the means to control men, General Cummings is not responsible for the victory over the Japanese, and Croft does not succeed in climbing Mount Anaka. Men and missions fail completely in *The Naked and the Dead*, a work described by John Aldridge as "a series of reductions to an absolute zero." [7] Mailer reverses his predecessors' principle of heroic collaboration and reduces the company of fighters to a set of hopeless individuals.

War as a subject for the epic novel was dealt a severe blow by *The Naked and the Dead*. Moreover, the relative peace in the world of the 1950s and 1960s created a condition in which the wanderings of the odyssey epic proved more appropriate than the fixed situation of the battle epic. Even in some novels in which World War II is still going on—novels such as *Catch-22* and *Across the River and into the Trees*—the individual's disengagement from the war, rather than the outcome of the war, is the principal concern. But most significant in the odyssey novels of the postwar period is the shift from a serious to a serio-comic point of view. Adopting the serious tone of the traditional epic did not seem possible to writers after World War II, and the successors of the rather grim Tom Joad and Robert Jordan are the half-humorous Henderson and the half-hilarious Yossarian. John Barth expresses the sentiments of his generation when he admits that copying traditional heroic patterns must be done a little ironically.[8] That Barth, Bellow, and others are still willing to copy heroic patterns without utterly destroying them may be taken as evidence of continued respect for the heroic tradition.

A spectrum representing the contemporary treatment of the odyssey motif would find Peter Matthiessen's *At Play in the Fields of the Lord* occupying one extreme, the serious; Barth's *The Sot-Weed Factor* at the other extreme, the comic; and Bellow's *Henderson the Rain King* at the center, keeping a perfect balance of the serious and the comic. In Matthiessen's novel a half-breed American Indian, Lewis Moon, returns to his people by way of a journey to South America, where he plunges into the jungle, lives among one of the few remaining tribes of American aborigines (one of Campbell's "isolated societies"), survives a fatal attack upon them from their white enemies, and returns—reborn—to life, a new Adam, "the only man beneath the eye of heaven." Moon's experiences in the South American jungle are very much like those of Henderson in Africa: he encounters the primitive life firsthand, witnesses the death of a wise old chief, comparable to King Dahfu, and is himself reborn from the chief's corpse. The way in which this is achieved is strikingly similar to Ishmael's delivery from the sea in *Moby-Dick*: the "death canoe" bearing the body of the chief down the river becomes the vehicle in which Moon escapes from both white men and Indians who seek to kill him. The encounter with death has the same effect upon Moon that it had upon Tommy Wilhelm, except that Moon is finally liberated by his experience.

> The Indian nation had grown old; he knelt down like a penitent and wept. He wept for Aeore and the doomed people of the jungle, and he wept for the last old leatherfaces of the Plains. . . . He wept and wept, and though toward the end he began to smile, he kept on weeping until at last he breathed a tremendous sigh and laughed quietly, without tears.[9]

Moon is a thoroughly serious person with a profound influence on all who meet him. To the Catholic priest in the last outpost of civilization, Moon is "A soldier of fortune, and of the classic type"; to the Indians he is the Great Spirit of the Rain, to the wife of a missionary he is a lover. In all these relations he is a credible enough character, who renews his life spiritually although he cannot succeed in rescuing his adopted people from catastrophe. The only comic strain in the book is supplied by Moon's companion, Wolfie, a roughneck adventurer who shares Moon's career up to the time Moon goes into the jungle; but Wolfie's hardheaded view of his strange companion's behavior is never allowed to threaten the basically serious tone of the book. Moon's spiritual rebirth is asserted against the rough humor of his friend, the light skepticism of the priest, and the phoney zeal of an evangelical missionary.

Ebenezer Cooke, the hero of *The Sot-Weed Factor*, also lives among American Indians, but his experiences are of quite a different order from Moon's. Far from making a journey to the mysterious origin of things, Eben goes to the New World in order to assume the office of "Poet and Laureate of the Province of Maryland" and to restore his legal right to his father's estate in the colony. His traveling companion is Henry Burlingame, who is searching for his father. The friends' quests are ridiculous, for Eben is but a poetaster, Maryland is but a "poor shitten" place not worth anyone's trouble, and the senior Burlingame turns out to be a renegade Indian chief. Russell Miller very ably establishes the "identification of Eben as an Odysseus-figure and his travels as an odyssey," Burlingame as the center of a Telemachan subplot, and the manner in which their adventures are related as mock-epic.[10]

Eben Cooke is in the tradition of the epicising poet and takes his place alongside of Presley in *The Octopus* and John Wickliff Shawnessy in Ross Lockridge's *Raintree County*. Each of these three poet-heroes is possessed by the ambition to write an epic poem celebrating some great American subject—Presley the early life of California, Shawnessy "the American Republic and its people," and Eben the early settlement in Maryland. Eben's poem was to be called the "Marylandiad" and promised to be the ultimate in epics: "An epic to out-epic epics: the history of the princely house of Charles Calvert. . . . the whole done into heroic couplets, printed on linen, bound in calf, stamped in gold."[11] Each poet eventually becomes disillusioned with his subject and writes something of a very different order from the epic he had intended. Finding Lord Baltimore's colony to be place of corruption, intrigue, and poltroonery, Ebenezer abandons his "Marylandiad" to write "a Hudibrastic exposé of the ills that had befallen him." It is a poem entitled "The Sot-Weed Factor." Presley responds to the economic exploitation of his fellow Americans with a bitter protest poem, "The Toilers." Similarly, the corruption of the city in the Gilded Age makes Johnny Shawnessy interrupt his labors: "The epic that he had meant to finish in the city was set aside, for into it had crept the City's own moral and artistic confusion." He begins a "verse-drama" in which a fierce contest is waged between a poet and a woman of the city, an obvious allusion to Johnny's affair with a temptress named Laura Golden. In the case of each poet, America is found wanting as a subject for an epic poem and the hero-poet fails to become either an epic hero or an epic poet. Presley's attempt to become a leader of the ranchers fails, Shawnessy leaves leadership to others, and Eben cuts a rather clownish figure.

But though the poet-heroes fail to write their epics, their novelist-creators do! The novel *Raintree County* is essentially the prose paraphrase of Shawnessy's abortive poem, just as *The Octopus* is the substitute for Presley's, and the *Sot-Weed Factor* a prose odyssey replacing Eben's heroic poem. The pursuit of the centuries-old ambition to produce the great American epic is itself the subject of these three novels, which in turn are themselves prose epics. In making their poets fail and then going on themselves to write epic novels, Norris, Lockridge, and Barth are suggesting that the novel, with its ready assimilation of epic materials and its easy irony, is a better modern inheritor of the epic tradition than narrative poetry.

Heroic possibilities are tested by the three writers within a framework that is both epic and novelistic. *The Octopus* is a battle epic conditioned by literary naturalism and *Raintree County* a double odyssey mixing epic portentousness with comedy. Lockridge manages to tell two odysseys, unfolding a Homeric *Odyssey* within a Joycean *Ulysses*: the adventures and wanderings of Shawnessy's entire lifetime are narrated in retrospect on a single day of his life on which he is pictured as "a traveller from dawn to darkness." And both odysseys are set within the context of an epic account of America's history in which the Civil War plays the most prominent part. Barth's mock-epic, in closely paralleling Homer's *Odyssey*, constitutes a more clearly ironical method to accomplish the same ends as Norris and Lockridge. The three works are variant expressions of disillusionment with the American ambition to produce an epic, and they find the same grounds for disillusionment: America's social shortcomings as a noble subject and as a place where heroes can thrive. Norris and Lockridge console themselves for the loss, Norris in a cosmic law of force, Lockridge in the mythic and Freudian mysteries of place and woman respectively. Barth allows himself refuge in the richest sort of comedy and parody, and yet persists in the search for an American hero and a proper field for his exploits. Heroism remains a distinct possibility for Barth even though the world in which it seeks to survive appears more and more absurd. In spite of his ineptitude, Ebenezer Cooke does have the courage to save the colony of Maryland from massacre, and he subscribes to a perfectly serious heroic ideal:

> there was something brave, defiantly human, about the passengers on this dust-mote who perished for some dream of Value. . . . their behavior was *quixotic*: to die, to risk death, even to raise a finger for any Cause was to pennon one's lance with the riband of Purpose, so the poet judged, and had about it the same high lunacy of a tilt with Manchegan windmills." (P. 732)

This recognition of the mixed quality of heroism, coming near the end of Eben's adventures, stands in contrast to his earlier facile understanding of the heroic as it appears in his plans for the epic he intended to write. Eben's conception of epic greatness, like Presley's, is corrected, but not overwhelmed, by experience. In Barth's next novel, *Giles Goat-Boy* (1966), colonial Maryland is replaced by a still more absurd community

—a computerized, worldwide college campus—yet his protagonist is a "professional hero" who sacrifices himself in the belief that something can be done to avert disaster to "all studentdom" (Western civilization) in the hour of the "gravest peril of its history." Another "Don Errant" like Eben, Giles was conceived by his creator to be "a protagonist . . . who would not be an anti-hero, but who, a little like Don Quixote, would take on heroic proportions." [12]

The latest variation in the Odyssean tradition finds Odysseus taking on the lineaments of Don Quixote. Giles, Ebenezer Cooke, Henderson, Shawnessy, and Brother are characters of whom it may be said, as Dostoevsky said of Don Quixote, that they are "noble only by being at the same time comic." [13] Each cherishes and protects from the erosion of unfavorable circumstances a traditional conception of heroism; each has to fight off his own occasional doubts and the skepticism of close associates. Ebenezer has the cynicism of Burlingame to resist; Giles has Dr. Spielman, who has no patience with "magical and transcendental" notions of heroism; Lewis Moon has Wolfie; Shawnessy, "Perfessor" Stiles; Prewitt, Sergeant Warden; and Henderson, Romilayu. Another recurrent element from the tradition established by Cervantes is the note of parody to be found in the exaggerated attempt of a contemporary figure to follow in the footsteps of a revered predecessor. Thus the hint in Henderson of masquerading as a Hemingway hero, the folly of Brother's attempt to imitate the Founder (or Booker T. Washington), the pity of Prewitt's trying to live up to the ideal of honor of his namesake Robert E. Lee, the vanity of Shawnessy and Ebenezer to write a great American epic poem comparable to Homer's, and the colossal ambition of Giles to be another Christ, or the "Grand Tutor," as he is called. In spite of irony and parody, however, epic heroism does not altogether die in the novels; it is simply made to operate in the context of a world in which absurdity is felt with more than usual keenness and the chances of humanity prevailing are not thought to be very high. To state this in terms of literary genre: a combination of the essential characteristics of the epic and the novel continues to be an effective means of expressing the ever-increasing ambiguities in the lives of modern man.

The cyclical renewal of life is the grand theme of American epic novels. It is a theme foreshadowed in *Moby-Dick*: out of destruction, rebirth; after death, the renewal of life; out of corruption, transcendence; after withdrawal, return. In *For Whom the Bell Tolls*, after the fiasco of the attack on the bridge, the life of the community is promised a renewal in another place when the guerillas flee with Maria, who has already been redeemed from corruption. Grinding economic exploitation forces the Joad family into the depths of human degradation, ending with the flood that obliterates all; but a new community, the whole exploited class, arises from the remnants of the old and will do battle another day. In *The Octopus* it is discovered that while cosmic law brings tragedy to some men, it saves others: the wheat lands, for the control of which some men die, produce an abundant enough harvest to "feed thousands of starving scarecrows on the barren plains of India." After facing death and deprivation, the two experiences he could not find in his American environment, Henderson resumes his normal life with new insights to guide him and renewed determination to make a success of it. Shawnessy's day of reminiscences awakens old specters but also confirms him in his lifetime quest: "he knew that he would be that dreamer, lost in darkness, lost and yet not lost, away and yet at home, forever awake and yet forever dreaming." Less hopeful than Henderson or

Shawnessy, the hero of *Invisible Man* still looks forward to the time when he will "shake off the old skin," emerge from his deepest Tartarus, and resume his search for "a socially responsible role to play." These endings are not glorious spectacles of greatness, not Hellenic funeral pomp, Roman triumphs, Christian martyrdom, nor New World promise of paradise. The scarred hero issues from an abject community and has only moderate chances of doing something noble. His glory is to be found, not especially in the cause of this or that reform or amelioration, but in the discovery of new life for both community and self; and his deeds, although they do not bring about actual delivery, are symbolical gestures of man's efforts to move in the direction of his yearning.

Notes

Introduction

1. *The American Novel and Its Tradition* (New York, 1957), p. 57.
2. *The English Epic and Its Background* (Oxford, 1954), p. 62.
3. *Trials of the Word* (New Haven, 1965), p. ix.
4. *The American Adam: Innocence, Tragedy, and Tradition in the Nineteenth Century* (Chicago, 1955), p. 144.
5. *Images of Truth* (New York, 1962), p. 8.

1—History and Definition

1. This and similar pronouncements may be found in Benjamin T. Spencer, *The Quest for Nationality* (Syracuse, 1957), p. 58.
2. Brian Wilkie, *Romantic Poets and Epic Tradition* (Madison, 1965), p. 10.
3. Stanley Vestal, *Kit Carson: the Happy Warrior of the Old West* (Boston, 1928), pp. 3–4.
4. Edward Dowden was probably the first to compare *Leaves of Grass* to classical epic. "The Poetry of Democracy: Walt Whitman," having first appeared in the *Westminster Review* of July 1871, may well have influenced Whitman, a year later, to call his collection of poems "an epic of Democracy." Three discussions of *Leaves of Grass* as epic are: Ferner Nuhn, "Leaves of Grass Viewed as an Epic," *Arizona Quarterly*, 7 (Winter 1951), 324–38; Roy Harvey Pearce, *The Continuity of American Poetry* (Princeton, 1961), pp. 69–83; James E. Miller, Jr., *A Critical Guide to* Leaves of Grass (Chicago, 1957), pp. 174–86.

5. *The Complete Writings of Walt Whitman* (New York, 1902), 9:228.

6. *A History of American Literature During the Colonial Time* (New York, 1897), 2:83.

7. *The Historical Novel*, trans. Hannah and Stanley Mitchell (London, 1962), p. 35.

8. *The Epic Strain in the English Novel*, 2nd ed. (London, 1963), pp. 74–116.

9. "Americanism in Literature," *Views and Reviews in American Literature, History and Fiction*, ed. C. Hugh Holman (Cambridge, Mass., 1962), p. 29.

10. Ibid., pp. 84–85.

11. J. V. Ridgely, *William Gilmore Simms* (New York, 1962), p. 41.

12. David Brion Davis, "The Deerslayer, a Democratic Knight of the Wilderness," *Leatherstocking and the Critics*, ed. Warren S. Walker (Chicago, 1965), pp. 90–91.

13. *Studies in Classic American Literature* (New York, 1923), p. 237.

14. *Herman Melville* (New York, 1950), p. 182.

15. *Love and Death in the American Novel*, rev. ed. (New York, 1966), p. 380.

16. *Complete Writings*, 5:254.

17. *The American Adam*, pp. 188, 141. The same dark impression was carried away from Homer by Goethe, who wrote to Schiller in 1803: "From Homer and Polygnotus I every day learn more clearly that in our life here above ground we have, properly speaking, to enact Hell." Matthew Arnold quoted this in "On Translating Homer" (1861).

18. *The Lost Image of Man* (Baton Rouge, 1963), p. 16.

19. "Epic Poetry" was first delivered as a lecture to the Salem Lyceum in 1837 and published two years later in Very's *Essays and Poems*.

20. Wilkie, *Romantic Poets and Epic Tradition*, p. 60.

21. "Biography," *Critical and Miscellaneous Essays* (New York, 1904), 3:51–52.

22. Translation of Dorothy Bussy (New York, 1955), p. 397.

23. This was part of Ellison's acceptance speech for the

National Book Award in 1953, reprinted in *The Crisis*, 60 (1953), 157–58.

24. *Thackeray and the Form of Fiction* (Princeton, 1965), pp. 165–66.

25. Ibid., p. 7.

26. *The Historical Novel*, p. 129.

27. *Thomas Hardy: A Critical Study* (New York, 1927), pp. 111, 104.

28. Greene, *The Descent from Heaven* (New Haven, 1963), pp. 11–12; Tillyard, *The Epic Strain in the English Novel*, p. 138.

29. Tillyard, *The Epic Strain in the English Novel*, pp. 15–17; Langer, *Philosophy in a New Key*, (New York, 1962), p. 169.

30. *Faulkner in the University*, ed. Frederick L. Gwynn and Joseph Blotner (Charlottesville, 1959; rpt. New York, 1965), pp. 74, 199.

31. *Light in August* (New York, 1932), p. 6.

32. *Look Homeward, Angel* (New York, 1929; rpt. New York, 1957), p. 159; *You Can't Go Home Again* (New York, 1940), p. 146.

33. *Anatomy of Criticism* (Princeton, 1957; rpt. New York, 1966), p. 137.

2 – The Octopus

1. *World's Work*, 5 (December 1902), 2904–6; reprinted in *The Responsibilities of the Novelist* (New York, 1928).

2. *Life in Letters of William Dean Howells*, ed. Mildred Howells (New York, 1928), 2:102–3.

3. "Editor's Easy Chair," *Harper's Magazine*, 103 (October 1901), 824; "Frank Norris," *North American Review*, 175 (October 1902), 774–75.

4. Hicks, *The Great Tradition* (New York, 1935), p. 171; Parrington, *Main Currents in American Thought* (New York, 1930), 3:333.

5. Norris, *The Octopus*, ed. Kenneth Lynn (Boston, 1958), p. 33.

6. John Curtis Underwood, *Literature and Insurgency* (New York, 1914), p. 165.

7. Garland, *Companions on the Trail* (New York, 1931), p. 168; Howells, "Editor's Easy Chair," p. 824.

8. Norris once visited a seed ranch in San Benito County, California; also, he may have been impressed by Edwin Markham's poem "The Valley," which was printed in *The Man with the Hoe, and Other Poems* (1899) at the very time that Norris was working on *The Octopus*:

> I know a valley in the summer hills,
> Haunted by little winds and daffodils;
> Faint footfalls and soft shadows pass at noon;
> Noiseless, at night, clouds assemble there;
> And ghostly summits hang below the moon—
> Dim visions lightly swung in silent air.

9. *Themis* (Cambridge, Mass., 1912; rpt. Cleveland, 1962), p. 522.

10. Sir James Frazer, *The New Golden Bough*, ed. Theodor H. Gaster (New York, 1964), p. 433. As D. Streatfeild defines the Demeter-Persephone myth, "Mother and daughter are one, each forever transforming herself into the other" (*Persephone: A Study of Two Worlds*, London, 1959, p. 161).

11. "Kore," *Essays on a Science of Mythology*, trans. R. F. C. Hull (New York, 1963), p. 130.

12. Visionary maidens who finally take on fleshly form are common enough to Romantic poets. In Shelley's *Epipsychidion*, for example, Emily Viviani emerges from the flower garden:

> I stood, and felt the dawn of my long night
> Was penetrating me with living light:
> I knew it was the Vision veiled from me
> So many years—that it was Emily
>
> (ll. 341–44)

More readily available to Norris was Hardy's *Tess of the D'Urbervilles*, in which Angel Clare beholds Tess under the two different aspects of ordinary milkmaid and "visionary essence of woman," or Demeter. Both men are taken with the lips of their sweethearts, Clare with "that little upward lift in the middle of her red top lip" and Vanamee with "the enchanting fulness of her lips." Tess is drawn to Clare's lute-playing in an "uncultivated" garden, just as Angéle's daughter is drawn by Vanamee's psychic call in an abandoned seed ranch. The imagery of rank vegetation and pollination is associated with Tess as with Angéle, except that Hardy's imagery is much coarser than Norris's. When her death appears inevitable, Tess implores Clare to take her young sister, Lizu-Lu, saying, "She has all the best of me without the bad of me [by which is meant she has not been tainted by rape] and if she were to become yours it would almost seem as if death had not divided us. . . ." It seems likely that a good deal of Hardy went into the making of both Angéle and Hilma Tree.

13. *The New Golden Bough*, pp. 395–96, 432–33.

14. Grant C. Knight, *The Strenuous Age in American Literature* (Chapel Hill, N. C., 1954), p. 44.

15. *Love and Death in the American Novel*, rev. ed. (New York, 1966), p. 384.

16. Quoted in Franklin D. Walker, *Frank Norris: A Biography* (New York, 1963), p. 262.

17. "Frank Norris," p. 774.

18. Harry Hartwick, *The Foreground of American Fiction* (New York, 1934), p. 64.

3 – The Grapes of Wrath

1. "A Neglected Epic," *The Responsibilities of the Novelist* (New York, 1928), p. 281.

2. *The Grapes of Wrath* (New York, 1939), p. 264.

3. Harry T. Moore, *The Novels of John Steinbeck* (Chicago, 1939), p. 71.

4. Steinbeck's Emersonian transcendentalism is carefully worked out by Peter Lisca in *The Wide World of John Steinbeck* (New Brunswick, N. J., 1958), pp. 168–69.

5. See H. Kelly Crockett, "The Bible and *The Grapes of Wrath*," *College English*, 24 (December 1962), 197; Charles C. Dougherty, "The Christ Figure in *the Grapes of Wrath*," ibid., p. 226.

6. See John E. Hart, "*The Red Badge of Courage* as Myth and Symbol," *University of Kansas City Review*, 19 (Summer 1953), 249–56.

7. *John Steinbeck* (New York, 1961), p. 107.

8. Ibid., p. 37.

4—For Whom the Bell Tolls

1. "An American in Spain," *The Partisan Reader*, ed. William Philips and Philip Rahv (New York, 1946), p. 643.

2. *The Complete Writings of Walt Whitman* (New York, 1902), 5:253.

3. *Hemingway: The Writer as Artist* (Princeton, 1956), p. 248.

4. The symbolism of wheat in *For Whom the Bell Tolls* is discussed by Melvin Backman in "Hemingway: The Matador and the Crucified," *Modern Fiction Studies*, 1 (August 1955), 2–11.

5. See C. M. Bowra, *Heroic Poetry* (London, 1961), pp. 482–84.

6. *The Lost Image of Man* (Baton Rouge, 1963), p. 32.

7. *Hemingway*, p. 247.

8. Ibid., p. 248.

9. *Epic and Romance* (London, 1896; rpt. London, 1926), p. 5. Baker also reminds us of "other small and local holding actions which are stuck like gems in the web of history": the Battle of Concord, Horatio at the Bridge, and Leonidas at Thermopylae (*Hemingway*, p. 247).

10. Edward Fenimore, "English and Spanish in *For Whom the Bell Tolls*," *Journal of English Literary History*, 10 (1943), 73–86.

11. *The Song of Roland*, trans. Dorothy L. Sayers (Baltimore, 1957), p. 138.

12. *The Short Stories of Ernest Hemingway* (New York, 1953), p. 213.

13. *For Whom the Bell Tolls* (New York, 1940), p. 471.

14. *Across the River and into the Trees* (New York, 1950), pp. 228–29.

15. *The Old Man and The Sea* (New York, 1952), p. 11.

5—Bellow's Odysseys

1. *Seize the Day* (New York, 1956), p. 118.

2. *Radical Innocence: Studies in the Contemporary American Novel* (Princeton, 1961), p. 315.

3. Irving Howe, *New Republic*, 151 (September 19, 1964), 21–26.

4. *Herzog* (New York, 1964), pp. 17–18.

5. Bellow majored in sociology and anthropology at Northwestern University and took a course in African ethnography from Melville Jean Herskovits, a noted anthropologist. Henderson lighly dismisses Richard Burton and John Hanning Speke—"we didn't see eye to eye about any subject" (*Henderson the Rain King*, p. 280)—but there is abundant evidence that Bellow made use of them and other anthropological sources in writing his novel. Instances of Bellow's debt to anthropologists are to be found in Genevieve Huber, "The Use of Anthropological Sources in *Henderson the Rain King*" (M.A. thesis, University of Maryland, 1967).

6. *Henderson the Rain King* (New York, 1959), p. 164.

7. Marcus Klein sees in Henderson's association with different animals a progress like that described in Zarathustra's first parable: "the spirit becomes a camel; and the camel, a lion; and the lion, finally, a child" (*After Alienation: American Novels in Mid-Century*, Cleveland, 1964, pp. 66–69).

8. In every face he encounters on Broadway, Tommy Wilhelm sees "the refinement of one particular motive or essence—*I labor, I spend, I strive, I design, I love, I cling, . . . I want*" (*Seize the Day*, p. 115).

9. *Waiting for the End* (New York, 1964) p. 98.

10. *The Hero with a Thousand Faces* (New York, 1949; rpt. Cleveland, 1964), p. 147.

11. *Mr. Sammler's Planet* (New York, 1970), p. 134.

6—Invisible Man

1. Ralph Ellison, *Invisible Man* (New York, 1947), p. 87.

2. *Writers at Work: The Paris Review Interviews*, 2nd ser., (New York, 1963; rpt. New York, 1965), p. 330.

3. See James M. Virden, "The Rebirth Motif in the Novels of Three Major Negro Novelists" (M.A. thesis, University of Maryland, 1963).

4. Rebirth imagery in *Huckleberry Finn* is studied by James M. Cox in "Remarks on the Sad Initiation of Huckleberry Finn," *Sewanee Review*, 70 (Summer 1954), 389–405; and Richard P. Adams in "The Unity and Coherence of

Huckleberry Finn," *Tulane Studies in English*, 6 (1956), 87–103.

5. A coarser version has *pisses* for *hisses*, *ass* for *pot*. Either Ellison bowdlerized the song or knew only the one version.

6. Near the end of Wright's *The Outsider*, Damon Cross, who is being pursued by the Communist Party, "longed for the shelter of a well-lighted place, something like a huge hotel lobby with throngs of people and hard, glaring electric bulbs shedding clarity and safety upon everything."

7. *After Alienation: American Novels in Mid-Century* (Cleveland, 1964), p. 145.

8. *The Negro Novel in America*, rev. ed. (New Haven, 1965), p. 202.

9. *Radical Innocence: Studies in the Contemporary American Novel* (Princeton, 1961), pp. 11–33.

10. Northrop Frye, *Anatomy of Criticism* (Princeton, 1957; rpt. New York, 1966), p. 322.

7 – The Continuing Tradition

1. "The Iliad," *Saturday Review of Literature*, 48 (March 27, 1965), 17.

2. Herman Melville, *Moby-Dick*, ed. Charles Feidelson (Indianapolis, 1964), p. 168.

3. James Jones, *From Here to Eternity* (New York, 1951), p. 596.

4. *The Hero with a Thousand Faces* (New York, 1949; rpt. Cleveland, 1964), p. 387.

5. *The Lost Image of Man* (Baton Rouge, 1963), p. 16.

6. *The Naked and the Dead* (New York, 1948), p. 497. In an interview with Harvey Breit, Mailer said: "The biggest influence on *Naked* was *Moby Dick*. . . . I was sure everyone would know. I had Ahab in it, and I suppose the mountain was Moby Dick" (*Writers Observed*, New York, 1956, p. 200).

7. *After the Lost Generation* (New York, 1951), p. 139.

8. "John Barth: An Interview," *Wisconsin Studies in Contemporary Literature*, 6 (Winter–Spring 1965), 6.

9. *At Play in the Fields of the Lord* (New York, 1965), p. 371.

10. *"The Sot-Weed Factor*: A Contemporary Mock-Epic," *Critique*, 8 (Winter 1965–66), 88–100.

11. John Barth, *The Sot-Weed Factor* (New York, 1960; rpt. New York, 1964), pp. 87–88.

12. "John Barth: A Truffle No Longer," interview by Phyllis Meras, New York *Times Book Review*, August 7, 1966, p. 22.

13. *Letters of Dostoevsky*, trans. E. C. Mayne (New York, 1917), p. 135.

Selected Bibliography

Abercrombie, Lascelles. *The Epic*. London, 1914.

Arvin, Newton. *Herman Melville*. New York, 1950.

Baker, Carlos. *Hemingway: The Writer as Artist*. Princeton, 1952.

Bowra, C. M. *Heroic Poetry*. London, 1961.

Brown, Herbert R. "The Great American Novel," *American Literature*, 7(1935), 1–14.

Campbell, Joseph. *The Hero with a Thousand Faces*. New York, 1949; rpt. Cleveland, 1964.

Chase, Richard. *The American Novel and Its Tradition*. New York, 1957.

Fiedler, Leslie. *Love and Death in the American Novel*. Rev. ed. New York, 1966.

————. *Waiting for the End*. New York, 1964.

Foerster, Donald M. *The Fortunes of Epic Poetry: A Study in English and American Criticism, 1750–1950*. Washington, D. C., 1962.

French, Warren. *John Steinbeck*. New York, 1961.

Friedrich, Werner P. *Outline of Comparative Literature*. Chapel Hill, N. C., 1954.

Frye, Northrop. *Anatomy of Criticism*. Princeton, 1957; rpt. New York, 1966.

Galloway, David D. *The Absurd Hero in American Fiction*. Austin, 1966.

Greene, Thomas. *The Descent from Heaven: A Study in Epic Continuity*. New Haven, 1963.

Gurko, Leo. *Ernest Hemingway and the Pursuit of Heroism*. New York, 1968.

Hartt, Julian N. *The Lost Image of Man*. Baton Rouge, 1963.

Hassan, Ihab. *Radical Innocence: Studies in the Contemporary American Novel*. Princeton, 1961.

Ingalls, Jeremy. "The Epic Tradition: A Commentary," *East-West Review*, 1 (Spring 1964), 42–69; 1 (Autumn 1964), 173–211; 1 (Winter 1965), 271–305.

Ker, W. P. *Epic and Romance*. London, 1896; rpt. London, 1926.

Klein, Marcus. *After Alienation: American Novels in Mid-Century*. Cleveland, 1964.

Levy, G. R. *The Sword from the Rock: An Investigation into the Origins of Epic Literature and the Development of the Hero*. London, 1953.

Lewis, C. S. *A Preface to Paradise Lost*. New York, 1943.

Lewis, R. W. B. *The American Adam: Innocence, Tragedy, and Tradition in the Nineteenth Century*. Chicago, 1955.

————. *Trials of the Word: Essays in American Literature and the Humanistic Tradition*. New Haven, 1965.

Lisca, Peter. *The Wide World of John Steinbeck*. New Brunswick, 1958.

Loofbourow, John. *Thackeray and the Form of Fiction*. Princeton, 1965.

Lukács, Georg. *The Historical Novel*. Trans. Hannah and Stanley Mitchell. London, 1962.

McNamee, Maurice B. *Honor and the Epic Hero: A Study of the Shifting Concept of Magnanimity in Philosophy and Epic Poetry*. New York, 1960.

Miller, Russell. "*The Sot-Weed Factor*: A Contemporary Mock-Epic," *Critique*, 8 (Winter, 1965–66), 88–100.

Mizener, Arthur. *The Sense of Life*. Boston, 1964.

Moore, Harry T. *The Novels of John Steinbeck*. Chicago, 1939.

Nuhn, Ferner. "*Leaves of Grass* Viewed as an Epic," *Arizona Quarterly*, 7 (Winter 1951), 324–38.

Raglan, Lord. *The Hero: A Study in Tradition, Myth, and Drama*. London, 1936.

Ridgely, J. V. *William Gilmore Simms*. New York, 1962.

Routh, H. V. *God, Man, and Epic Poetry: A Study in Comparative Literature*. Cambridge, 1927.

Spencer, Benjamin T. *The Quest for Nationality*. Syracuse, 1957.

Stanford, W. B. *The Ulysses Theme*. Oxford, 1954.

Tillyard, E. M. W. *The English Epic and Its Background*. Oxford, 1954.

————. *The Epic Strain in the English Novel*. London, 1958; rpt. London, 1963.

Walker, Franklin D. *Frank Norris: A Biography*. New York, 1963.

Wilkie, Brian. *Romantic Poets and Epic Tradition*. Madison, 1965.

Index